MAXWELL DOREY

2025

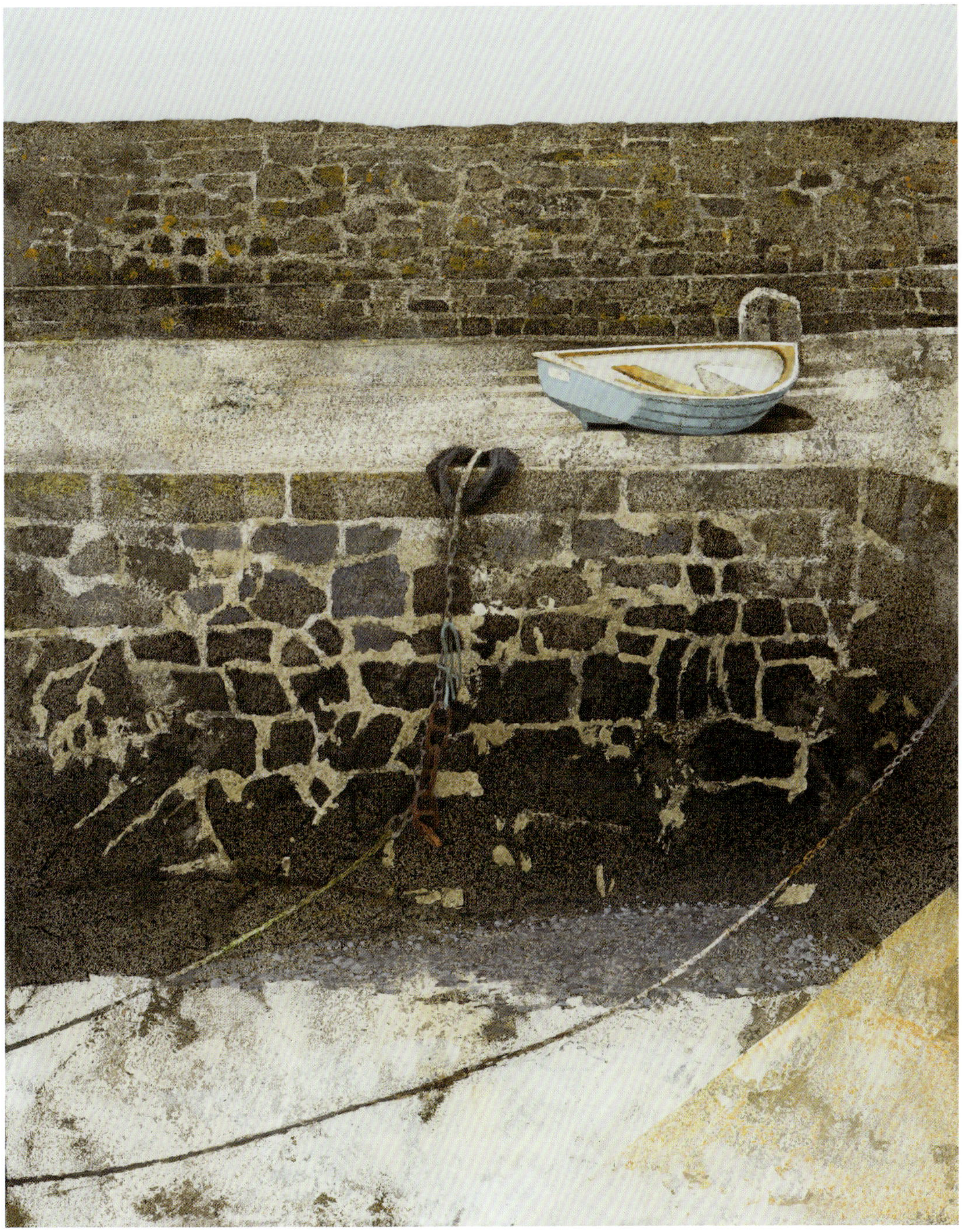

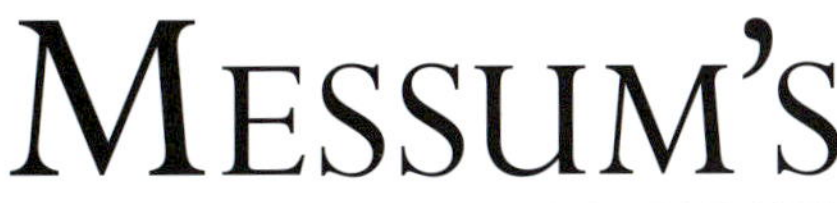

www.messums.com

12 Bury Street, St James's, London SW1Y 6AB   +44 (0)20 7287 4448   info@messums.com

davidmessumfineartltd

Introduction

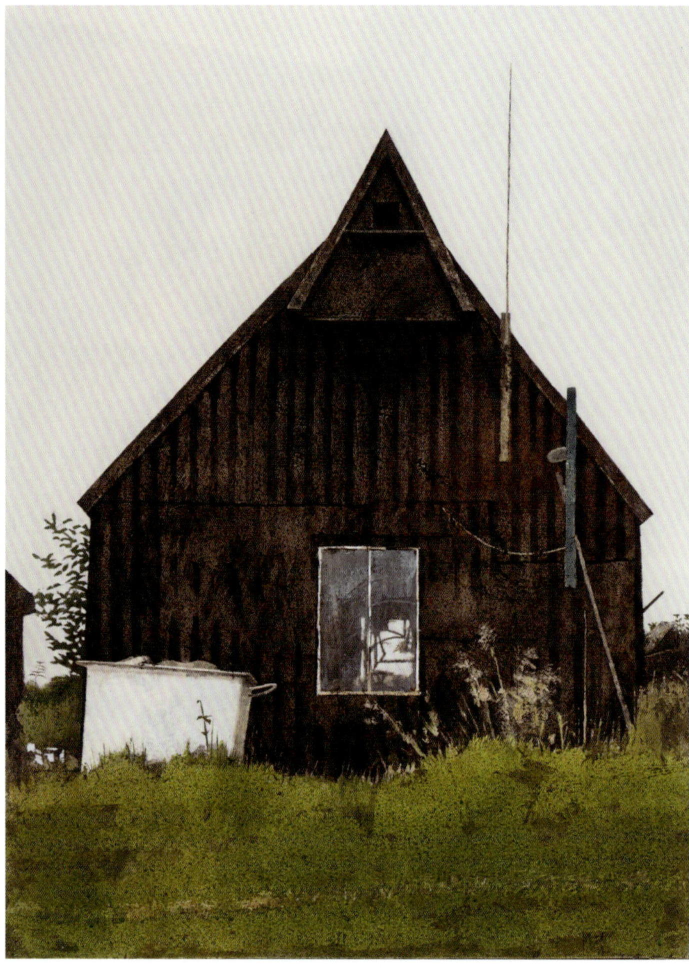

◀ 3 Fisherman's Hut, White Sky, Southwold
acrylic on canvas on panel
80 x 58 cms 31½ x 22⅞ ins

▶ 4 Quayside Boat, Morston I
acrylic on canvas on panel
122 x 98 cms 48 x 38⅝ ins

"I love to paint the old buildings near the harbour at Polperro. Many of these are white and I like the way they appear to be stacked up the valley sides like building blocks. I especially like the gable end on the inner harbour wall. It has a prominent, crisp shape, a bit like a block of cheese. You can see its age and history etched into its surfaces."

Max's words describe more than the surface of his paintings, they are a true expression of an authentic experience captured in decisive moments. Approaching the harbour village of Polperro from the water, he continues a tradition of artists, Frank Brangwyn (1867–1956) and Charles Napier Hemy (1841–1917) among the earliest of them, who came to discover the Cornish peninsular from the water's edge and to capture its characteristics from a perspective only few can either afford or endure. Being 'up close and personal' with his subjects forms not only one of the key allures of Max's pictures, but the foundation of his practice as a landscape painter and a firm element of his own personality as an artist.

Authenticity of character is in itself the basis of the school of naturalism to which the artist colonies of the nineteenth centuries adhered to. In the young rural artists of Cornwall, Norfolk, Yorkshire, Dumfries and Galloway, this naturalist tendency in painting that emerged in France and the Low Countries advanced itself in the abundantly textured environments of Newlyn, Falmouth, Staithes, Cullercoats and Kirkcudbright. As a painting nomad of sorts, Max has the luxury of capturing all of these places in one go. His most recent work, and subsequent journeys, have expanded the reach of his subject matter to encapsulate locations even more quaint and characterful than the last. Coastal towns and villages such as Portloe, Coverack and Flushing in the Southwest, Dungeness in the Southeast, Southwold and Brancaster in East Anglia, to Fylingthorpe and in the Northwest and beyond to the Isles of Mull in Scotland, each demonstrate Max's consistent ability to relate back to us hidden histories, or reacquaint us to ordinary objects that we may believe to already be accustomed to.

"Across the water from Falmouth, at the village of Flushing, there is an amazing harbour wall. It was built by Dutch engineers three hundred years ago and it looks as solid as the day it was built. The long stones are stacked vertically and interlock in an intricate way. I haven't seen anything quite like it. There is a sprinkling of orange lichen on the stones and you can see the tide lines across it. As soon as I saw the wall, I knew I had to paint it."

Max's enthusiasm for his humble subjects is, if it were even possible, more apparent in his recent works than ever before. In some curious way, his paintings of isolated objects

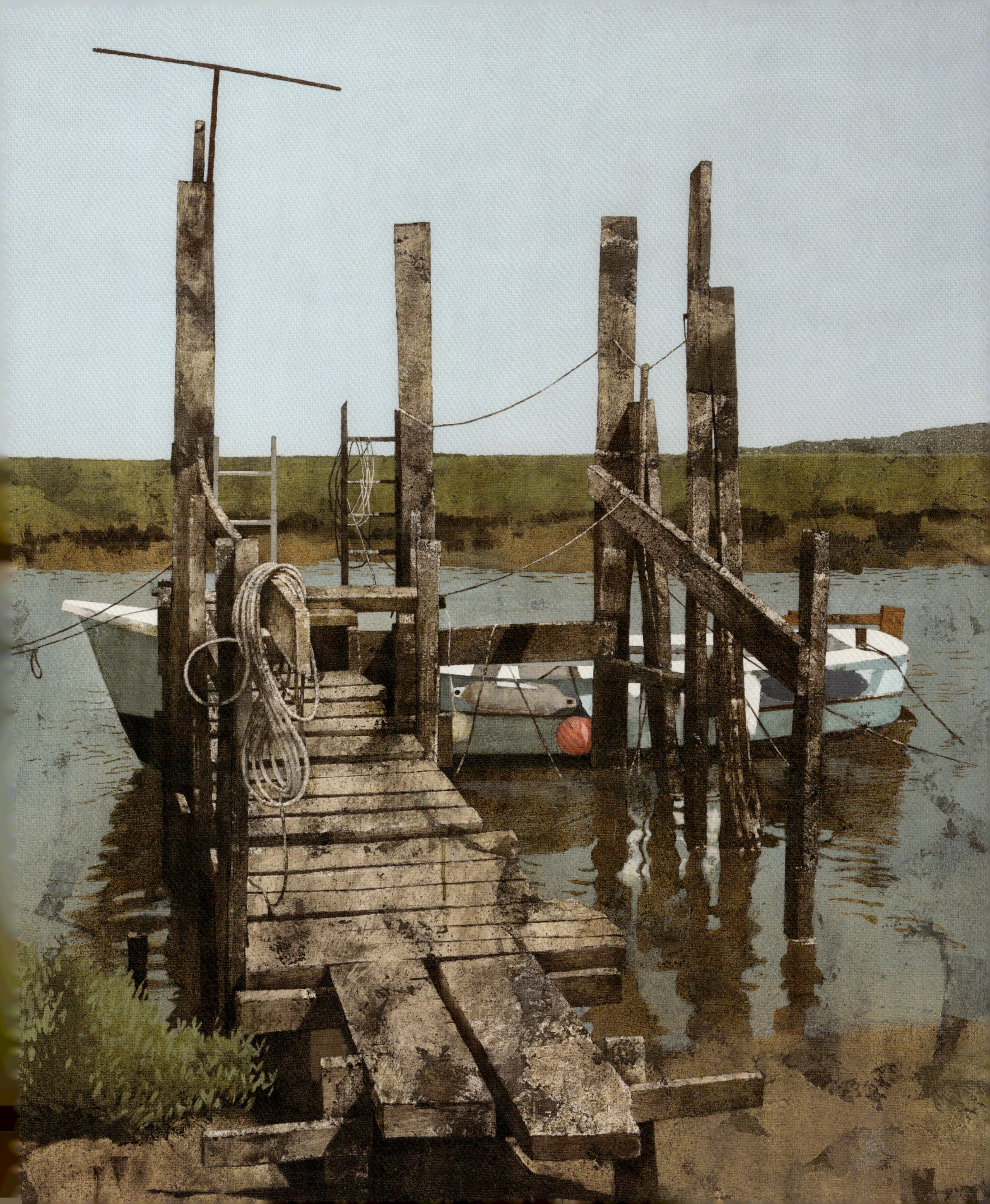

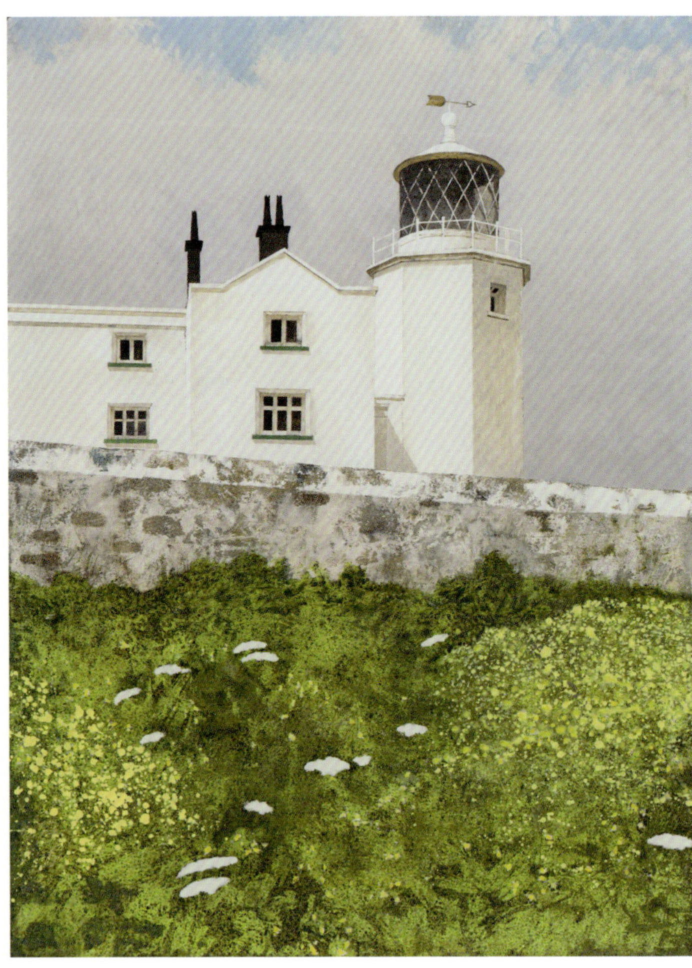

5 Lizard Lighthouse, Spring
acrylic on canvas on panel
74 x 55 cms 29¼ x 21½ ins

6 Mousehole Harbour Boats II
acrylic on canvas on panel
75 x 61 cms 29½ x 24 ins

7 Polperro Harbour III
acrylic on canvas on panel
83 x 61 cms 32½ x 24 ins

– boats at low tide, weatherworn quaysides, age-old gate posts, vigilant lighthouses or tumbledown potting sheds – seem to personify his carefully framed (in the visual sense) compositions and provide a narrative to the image, which is at once idiosyncratic to Max whist also expressing the vernacular of the region he is in.

This idea of regionalism is one that has followed Max's work for some time. Early works reflect the post-industrial, rural environment of his hometown. He describes Huddersfield in its fundamental terms, 'an industrial town in West Yorkshire, with sandstone buildings on the edge of the Pennine hills,' adding that these elements combined probably shaped him as a painter, as well as accounting for the gritty surfaces in his paintings. Local character provides the tone of his pictures, therefore a change in location provides the noticeable change of attitude and feeling of his pictures. Quite often, due to the lack of native examples available, the combination of subject matter and his technical treatment of his painted surface is compared to the work of Andrew Wyeth or Winslow Homer, two of the leading painters of rural north America during the years of the Great Depression. I considered this notion via one of their contemporaries Grant Wood, who's dual portrait, *American Gothic* (Art Institute of Chicago, Chicago) is often cited as the epitome of Regionalism in American painting and one whose title led me to think about Max's work in terms of a similar, let's call it, *Northern Gothic* representation of West Yorkshire.

The drystone walls, the gable ends, the crofters cottages stood starkly against crisp blue skies, or the boundless heights of snow clouds encroaching the moors, all provide

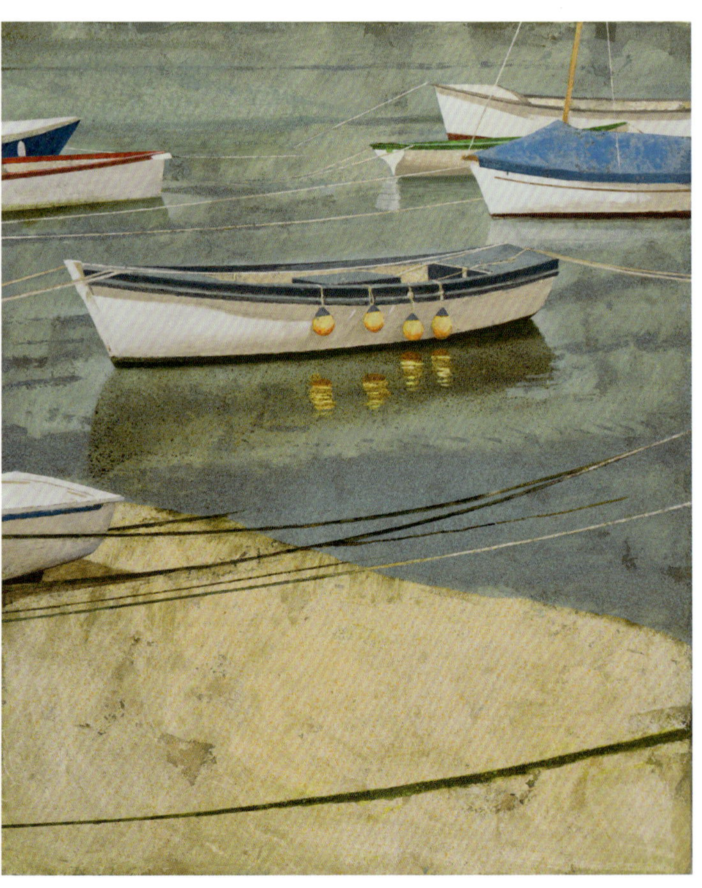

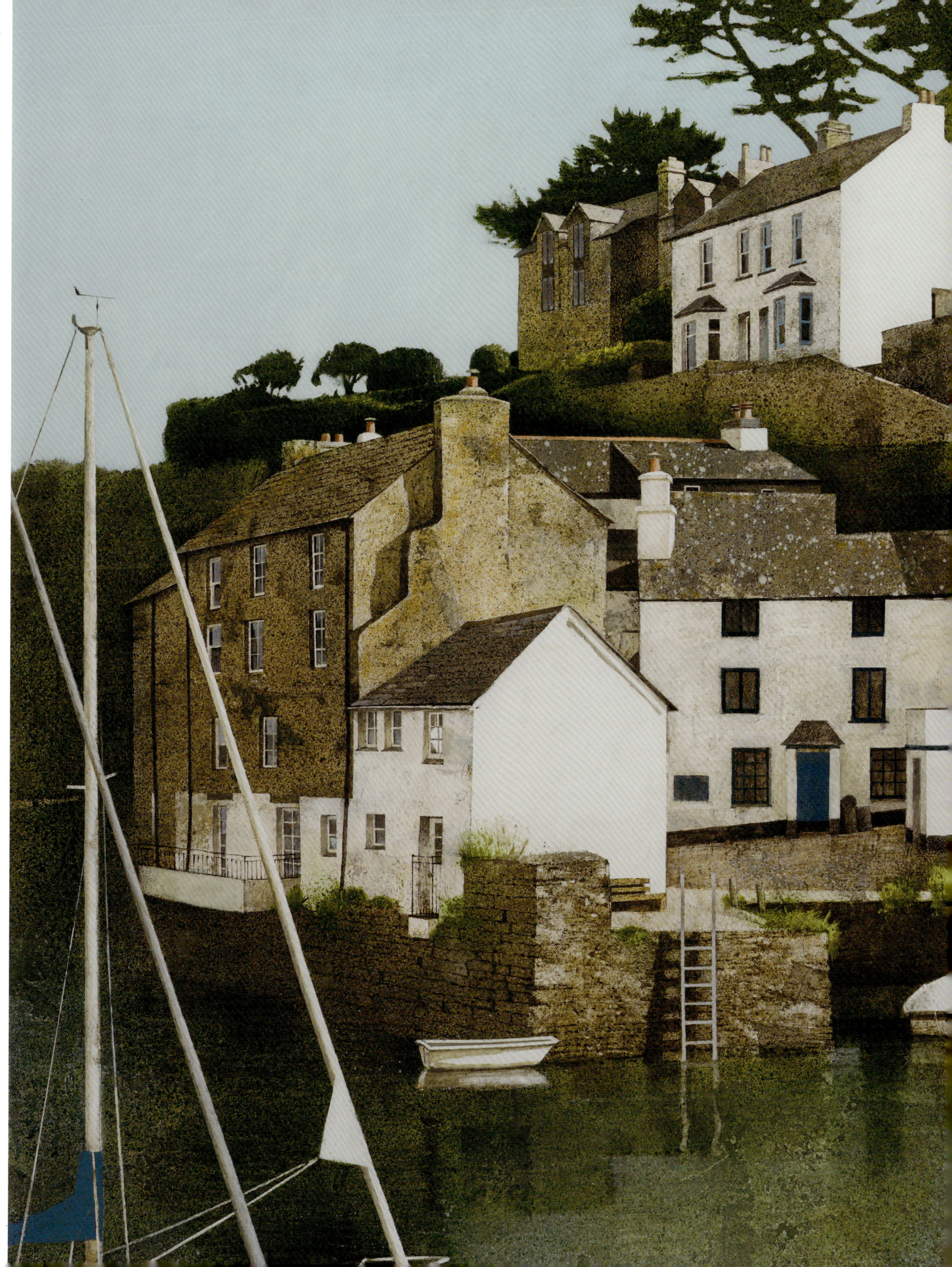

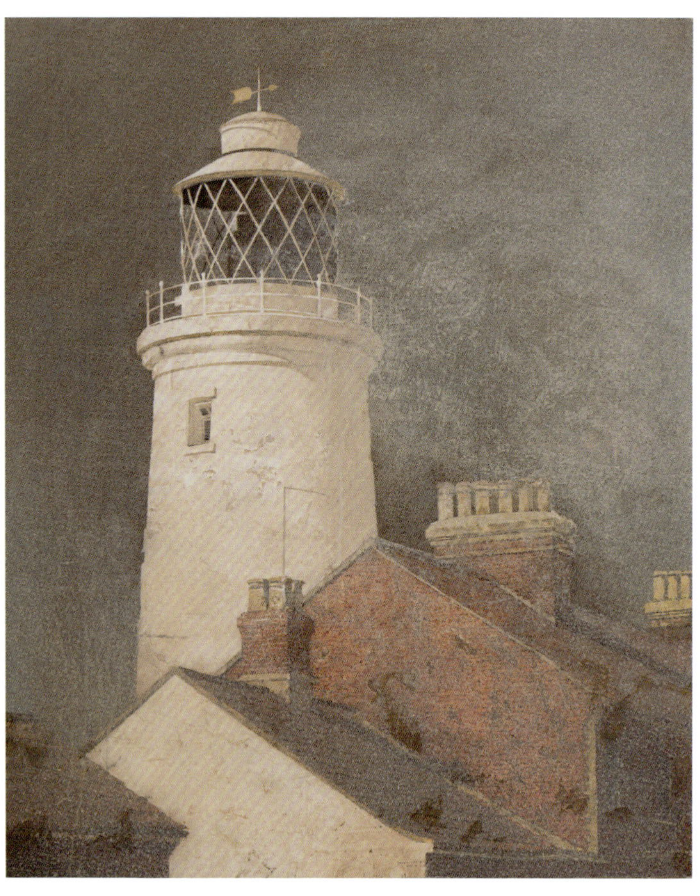

8 Sunshine and Rain, Southwold Lighthouse
acrylic on canvas on panel
76 x 61 cms 29⅞ x 24 ins

9 North Norfolk Quayside, Dusk
acrylic on paper
67 x 52 cms 26½ x 20½ ins

10 Polperro Harbour I
acrylic on canvas on panel
101 x 75 cms 39¾ x 29½ ins

a voiceless drama to the unpopulated landscapes which occupy the rich literary history of the area through authors such as Elizabeth Gaskell, Emily Brontë and Ted Hughes. Their 'Northern Gothic' doesn't really have a defined role in British art or its wider cultural fields, however these characteristics certainly conjure up in one's mind the rudiments of social isolation and post-industrial landscapes that often abound in the broader realms of bucolic Northern romanticism.

A far cry away from the bleak sobriety of Barry Hines' *A Kestrel for a Knave* (1968), Max breathes a new perspective of the roles played out by the cold comfort landscape of the Yorkshire moorlands, with the abandoned small-holdings and outhouses, or comely cottages and solemn churches which sparsely populate it in their minor roles. Consider *Woodland Ruin Near Haworth* (no. 59) or *Abandoned House above Marsden, II* (no. 32) in which our protagonists – both natural and man-made – engage with one another, sometimes leaning on each other like old friends or, perhaps, old enemies; worn out and weathered in equal measure. With a visual poetry evocative of an Old England concerned with T. S. Elliot, John Keats, and William Wordsworth, the landscape becomes a standalone character all of its own: one with a reverence for nature; luscious, sensuous and deeply emotional, enticing the wanderer to explore its hidden depths further.

Perhaps it is this austere concern for natural elements and their proximity with the human-built environment which amplifies those romantic echoes of rural naturalism in Max's carefully considered coastal landscapes. As an admirer of the work of John Constable (1776–837), there are inevitable temperamental cadences in the colour tone of certain works

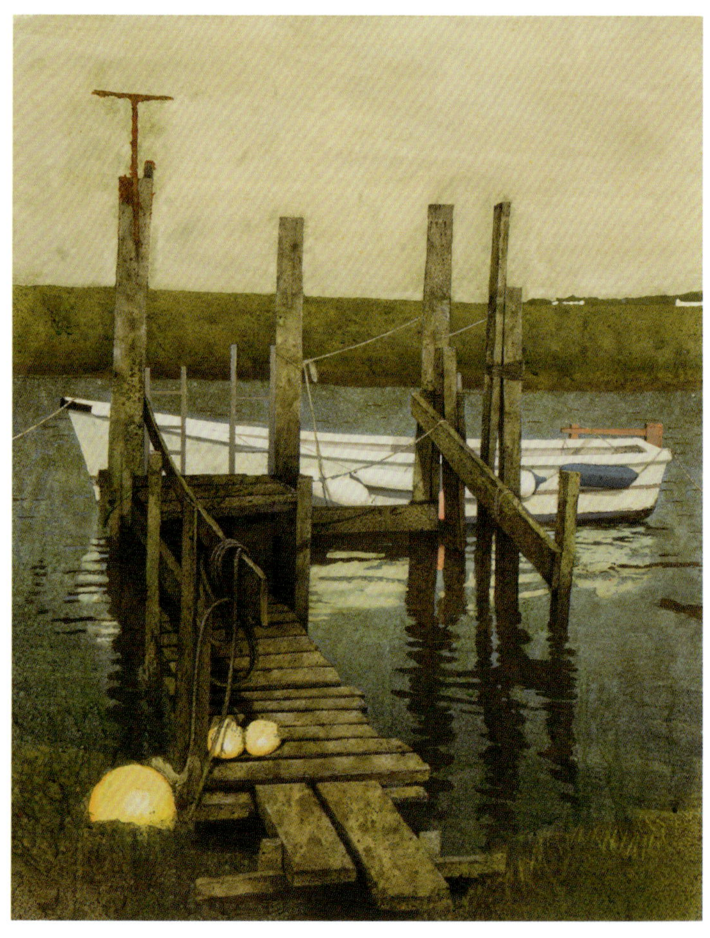

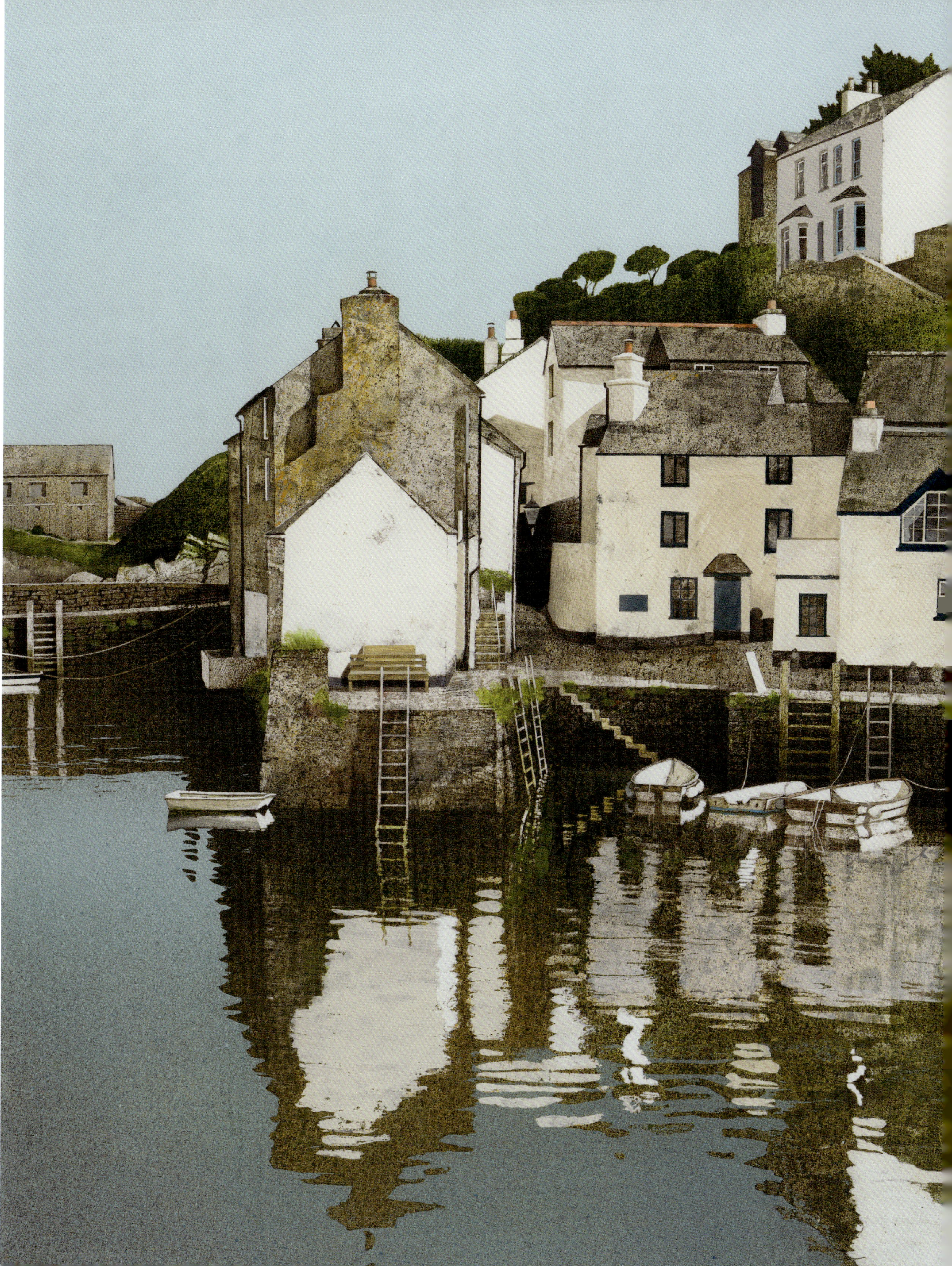

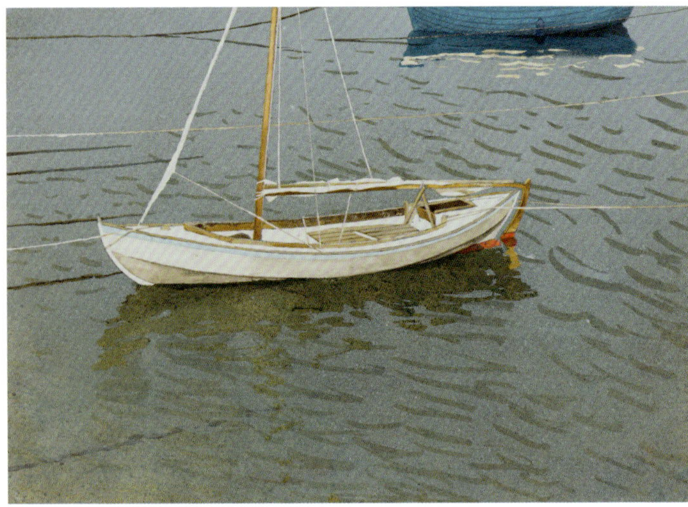

◀ 11 Mousehole Harbour Boats IV
acrylic on paper
50 x 69 cms 19½ x 27 ins

▼ 12 Mousehole Harbour Boats III
acrylic on paper
51 x 67 cms 20 x 26½ ins

▶ 13 Coverack Harbour Wall
acrylic on canvas on panel
49 x 61 cms 19¼ x 24 ins

the further Max travels along the coast which refer back to history. Max admits that you can see the '*warm brownish grounds with greens laid on top and then white highlights coming through*' are in direct lineage – if not homage – to the earthiness that exemplifies Constable's work. Max himself begins with a mid-tone, or warmish ground, and builds up in lighter and darker tones from there to invoke 'the freshness of a coastal impressionism.'

The placidity found in Max's views at Morston (nos. 4, 26) may not match that of the atmospheric drama played out in many of Constable's own views of Norfolk, but the solicitude he provides his chosen subject, the small boats moored up by the quay, is more than comparable in its sense of representation and handling. By delineating these humble objects against the natural front and back drop of the waterways, Max draws into soft focus ordinary objects which accent the voice of the coastal region.

One could bring L. S. Lowry (1887–1976) into the fold in regard to his rigid, set-like architecture emphasised only by the vacant skies they foreground, but it would be better to mention another great Northern artist, whose early influence on Max when he was a student, is more personal and poignant in our scheme of his structural perception of commonplace objects.

It was with the late David Blackburn (1939–2016) from whom Max 'soaked up like a sponge' his abilities to draw from life over 30 years ago. Whilst his own abilities and vision have evolved since then, Max credits Blackburn's influence for the semi-abstracted quality of his work, and his continuing interest in surface texture. A Slade trained artist-draughtsman, Max was originally a printmaker, the textural thread of which runs through the figurative subjects in his formative work, much inspired in content by Slade luminaries such as Stanley Spencer, William Coldstream, and Euan Uglow, eventually winding his way into his architectural studies and producing abstracted, industrial structures in the print workshop. 'As a student I would sometimes go out and draw the gasometers behind Kings Cross, an area which looked completely different then, and on home visits, I would sometimes meet up with David, if he was around, and go drawing in the landscape.'

There is, therefore, a personal history to Max's landscapes. It isn't simply enough to be there, but to exist in them, to occupy them, to camp under the trees and the meet the shore at the water's edge in order to understand them and their human histories more fully.

> *'Going to the places I paint, being there, standing there, the physicality of place, it gives me a sense of history. They are real places where real people lived and did real things. If you look closely, there are signs*

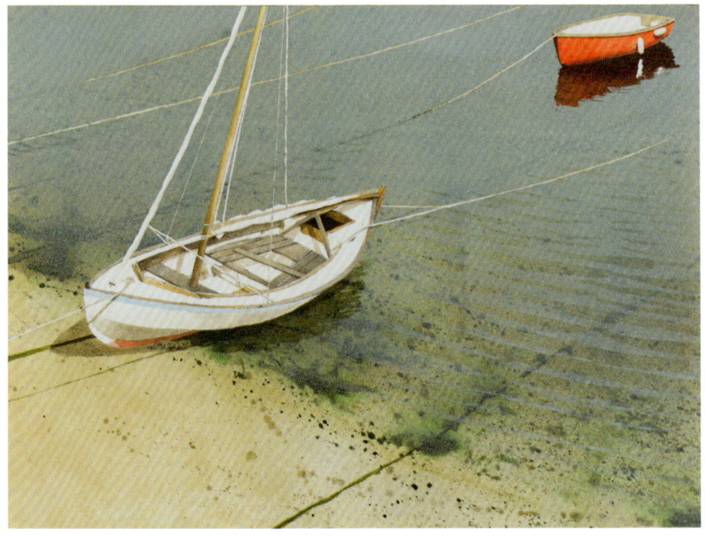

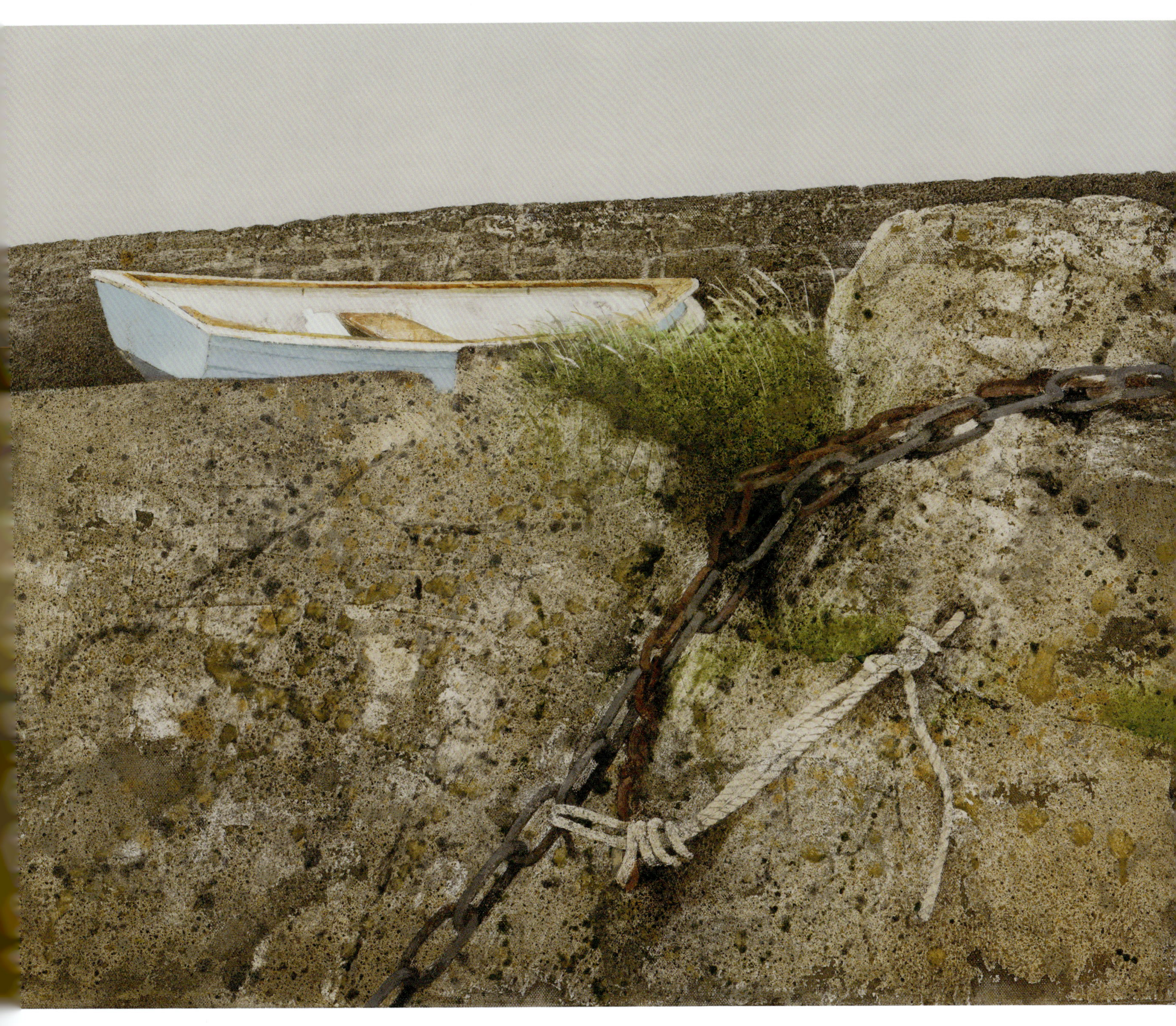

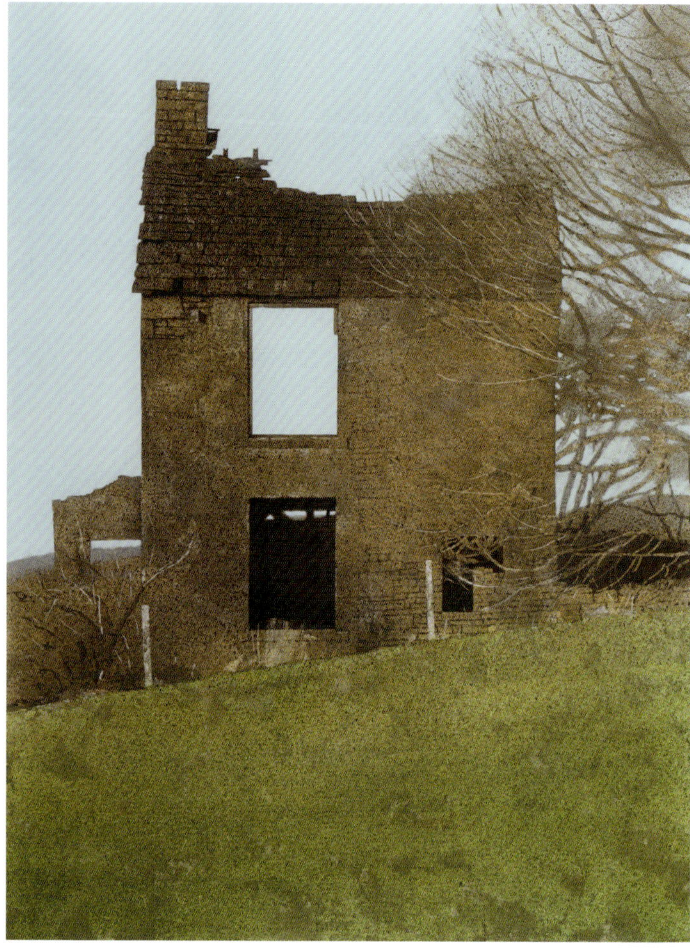

◀ 14 Old House Façade near Rawtenstall
acrylic on canvas on panel
83 x 61 cms 32½ x 24 ins

▼ 15 Church with Holly Tree, Fylingthorpe
acrylic on canvas on panel
83 x 61 cms 32½ x 24 ins

▶ 16 Quayside Reflection, Noss Mayo II
acrylic on canvas
102 x 75 cms 40 x 29½ ins

and traces of past lives. Looking at an old building and what it is built on and the shape of it can tell something about the character of the people who built it. It's like looking into the past.'

Through this temporal lens there is something about his 'remembered places' that appear timeless. This, he reminds us, is down not only to elements you do see in his paintings, but what you don't see. Mobile phone masts, parking ticket machines, bollards, litter bins, barriers, signage, cash point machines, cars and high fencing, both plastic and metal, none of which does he choose to include in his pictures. This is not by the process of erasure, but the keen angling and framing choices that he makes in order to exclude them. No simple task in the contemporary sense. As Max rightly says, "They are everywhere, even Cornwall."

The element of retrospection he puts down to 'getting a bit older,' but this, despite being a very Northern attribute, is a major facet of the universality of his pictures. They provide a sense of connecting the past with the present in a way which provides their familiarity regardless of whether you've ever set foot near their subject, experiencing for yourself the clarity of light reflecting off the water and the boats; the way the greens of the trees, which grow down to the shore, are made luminous in the water; or gazing up for the first time, at that unusual gable end that looks 'a bit like a block of cheese'.

Patrick Duffy
Archivist for David Messum Fine Art

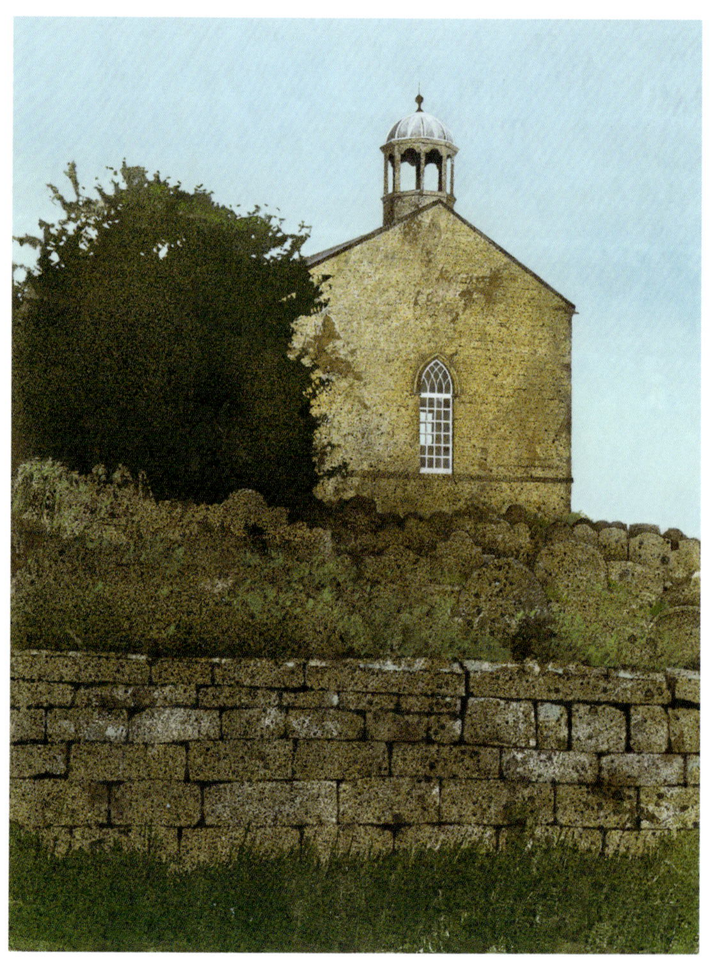

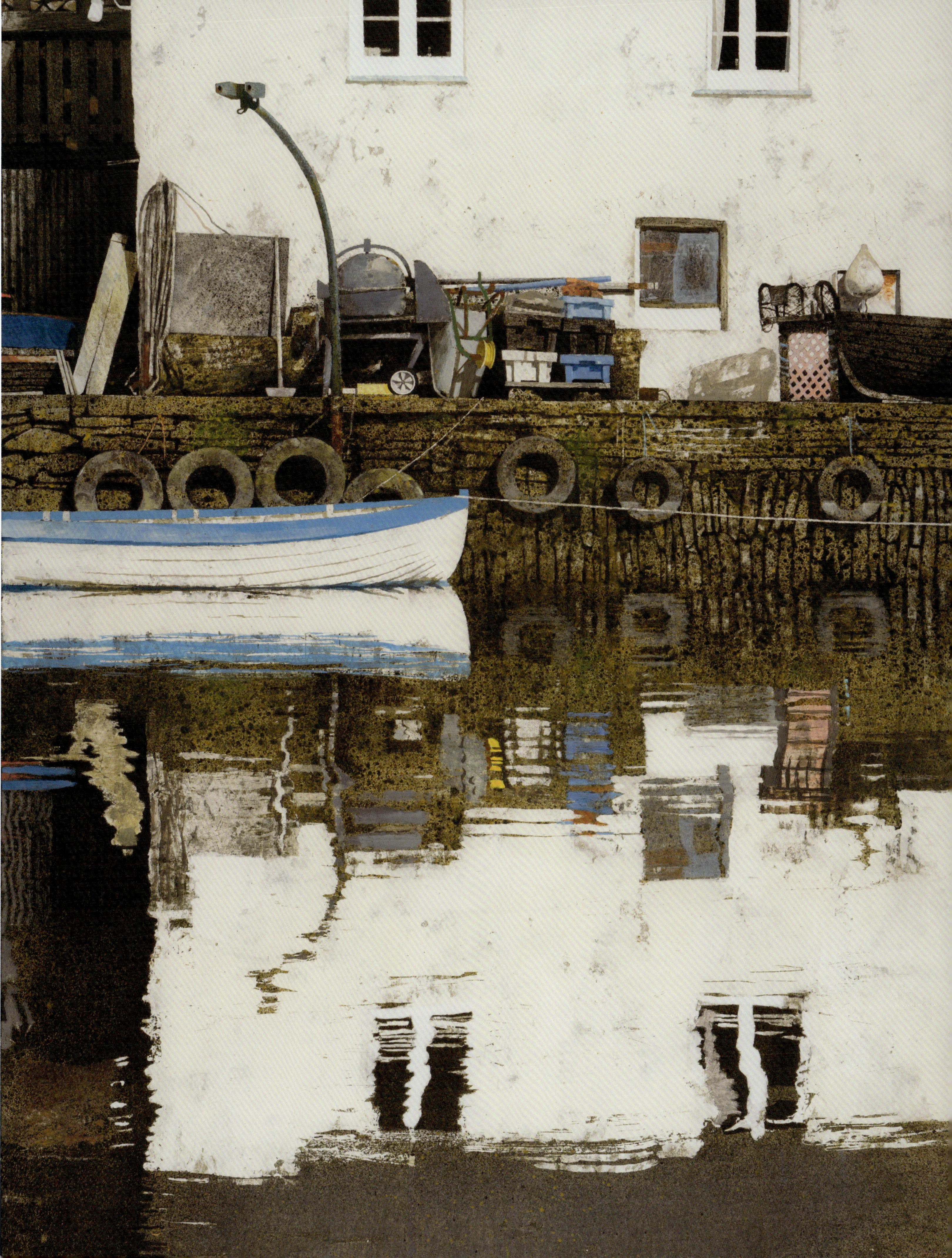

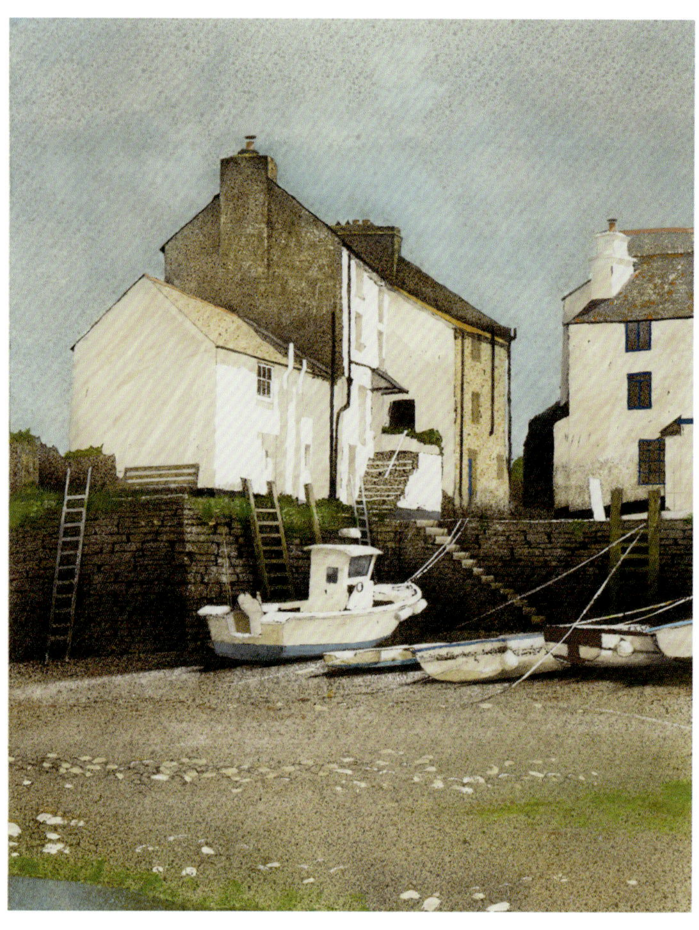

◀ 17 Polperro Harbour, Low Tide
acrylic on paper
67 x 52 cms 26½ x 20½ ins

▼ 18 Boathouse Reflection, Newton Ferrers I
acrylic on canvas
83 x 65 cms 32½ x 25½ ins

▶ 19 Fal Oyster Boat, Mylor Harbour
acrylic on canvas on panel
77 x 61 cms 30½ x 24 ins

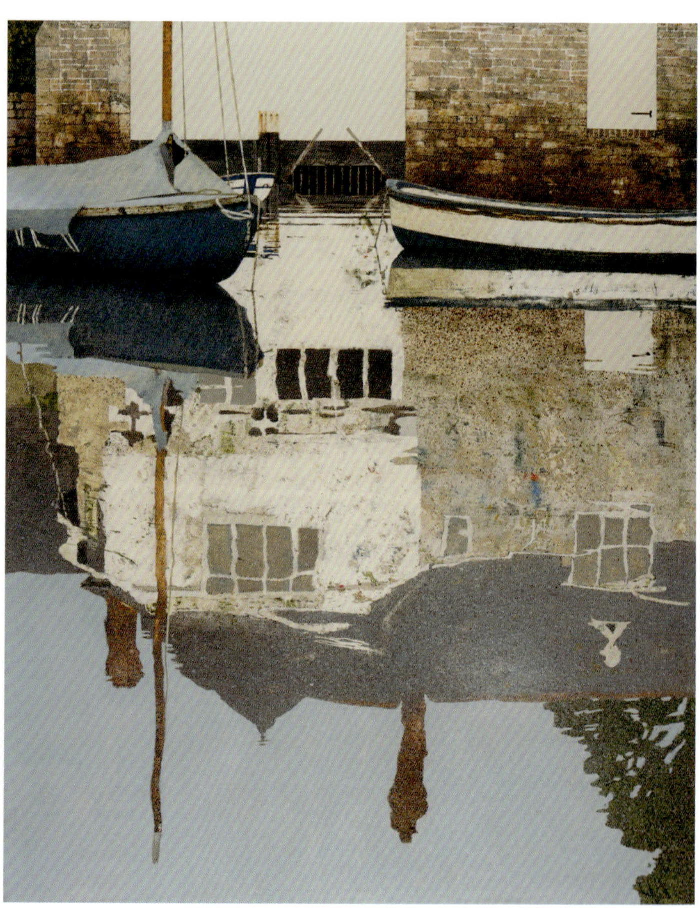

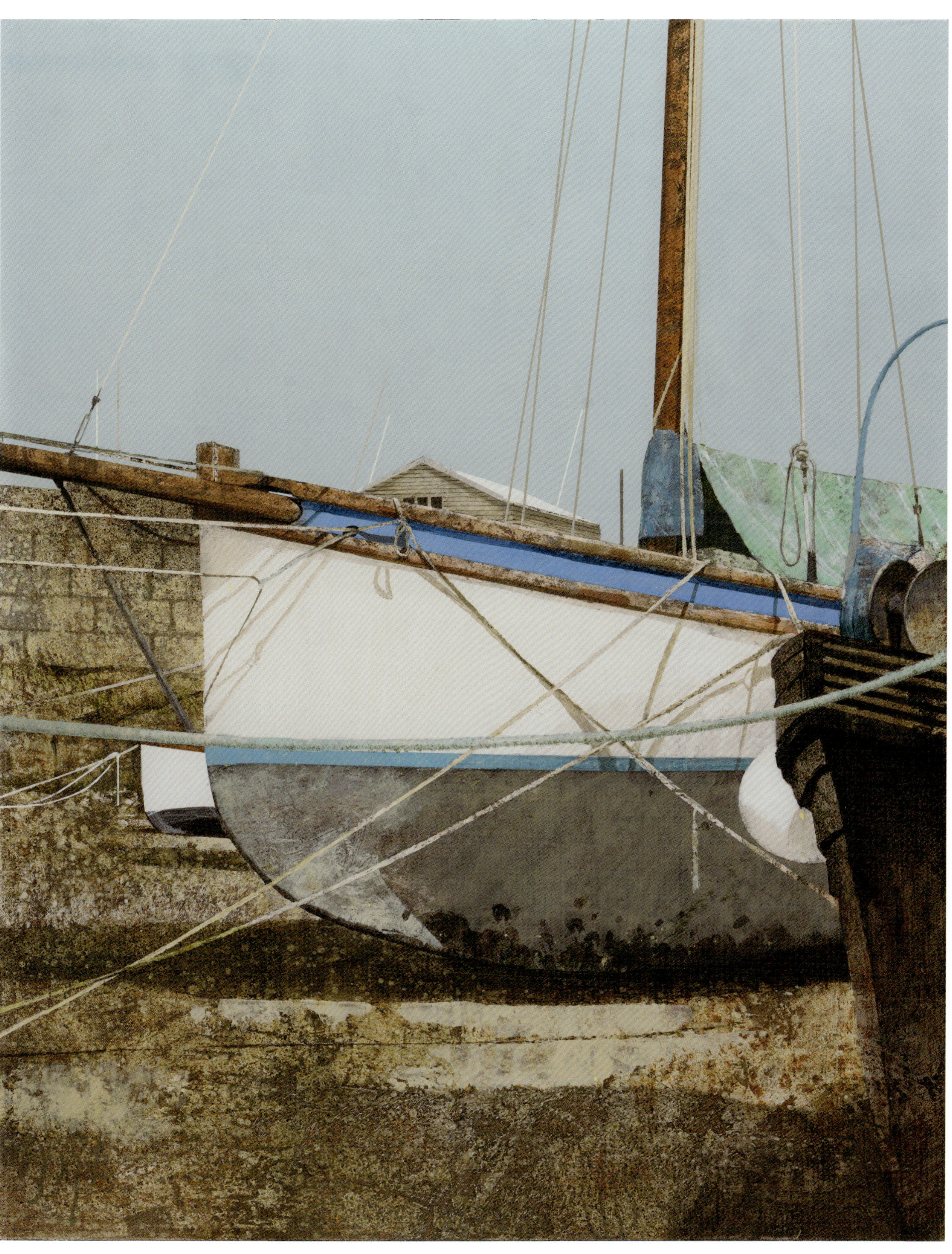

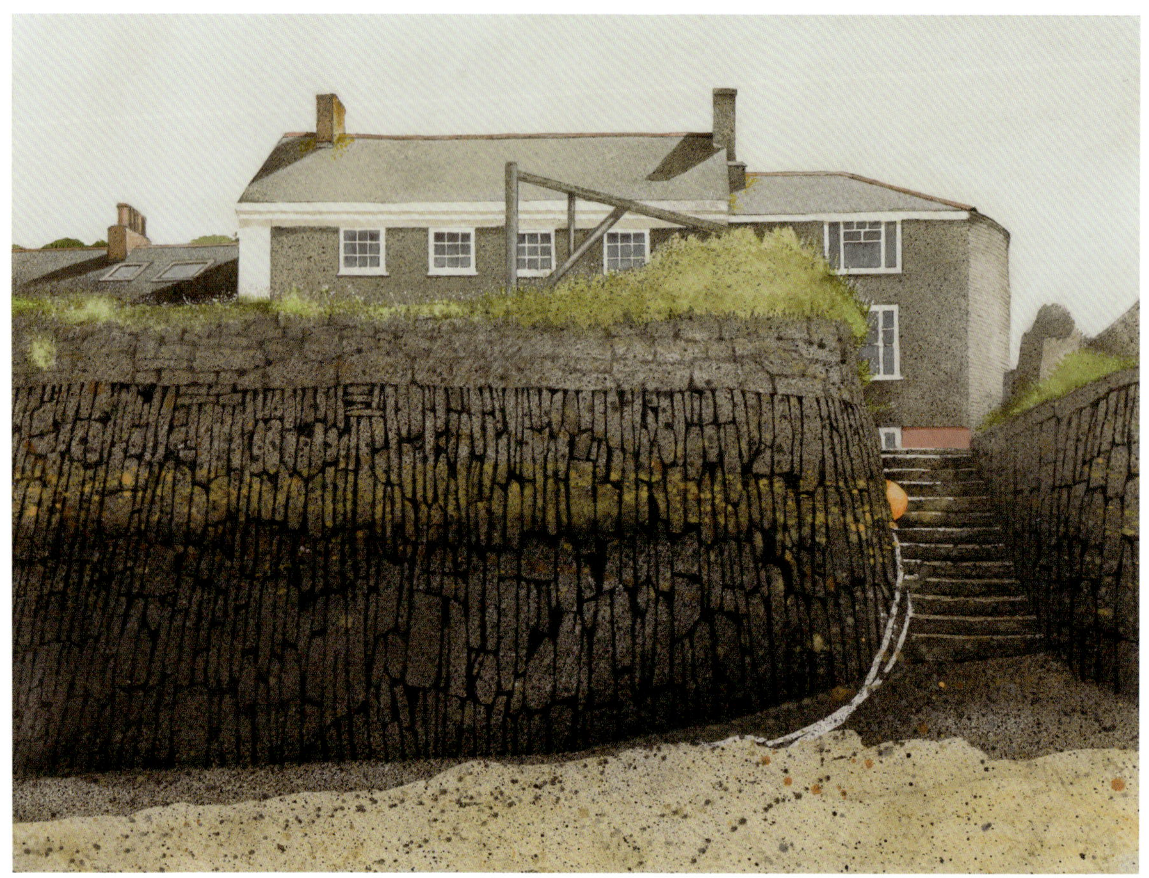

20 Flushing Harbour Wall

acrylic on paper
52 x 67 cms
20½ x 26½ ins

21 Boat Reflections at Newton Ferrers

acrylic on paper
52 x 69 cms
20½ x 27 ins

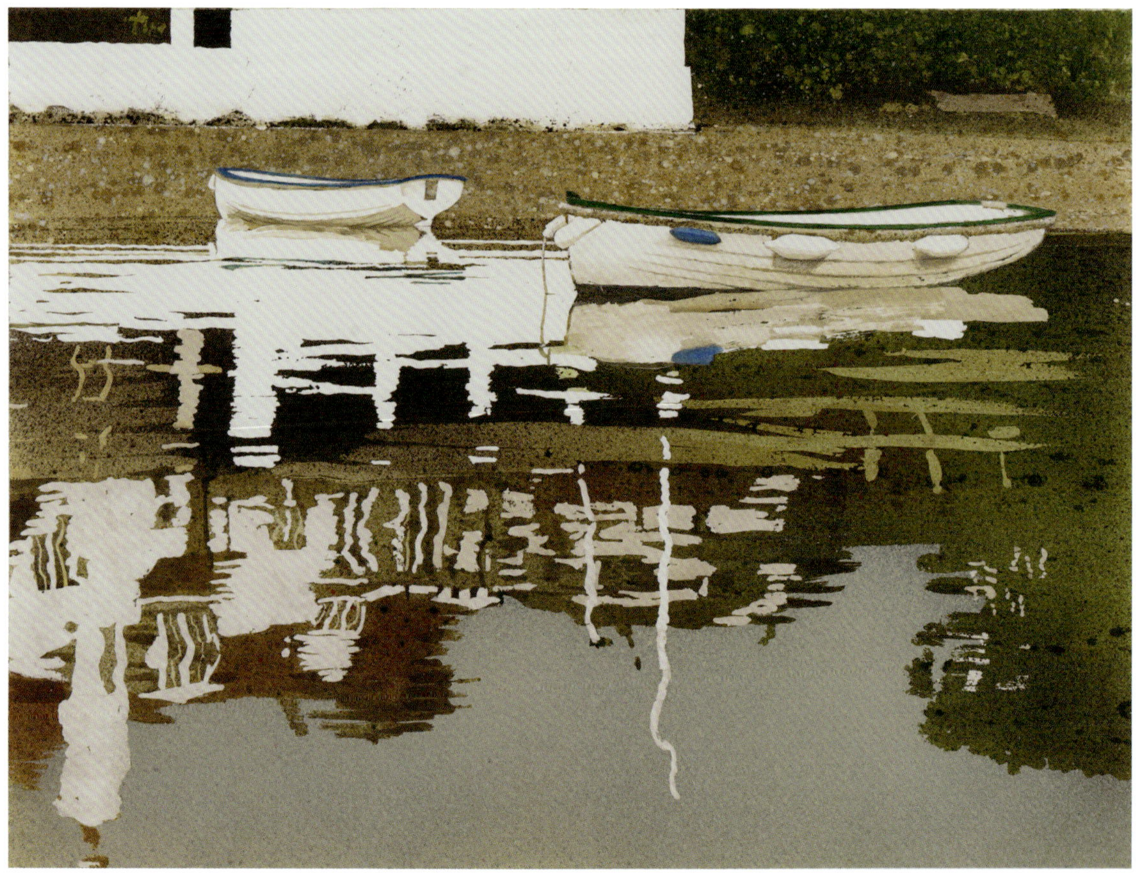

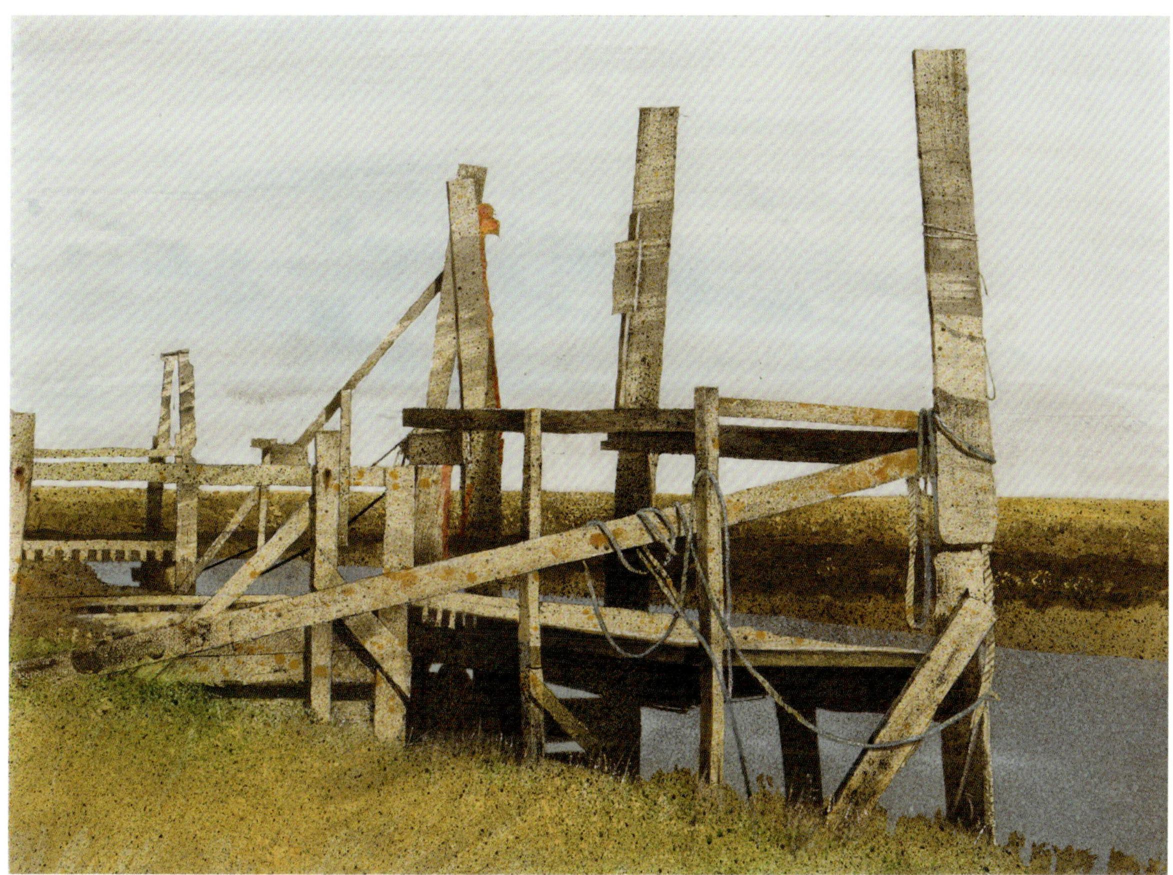

22 North Norfolk Quayside
acrylic on paper
50 x 67 cms
19½ x 26½ ins

23 Portloe, Bright Morning II
acrylic on paper
50 x 69 cms
19½ x 27¼ ins

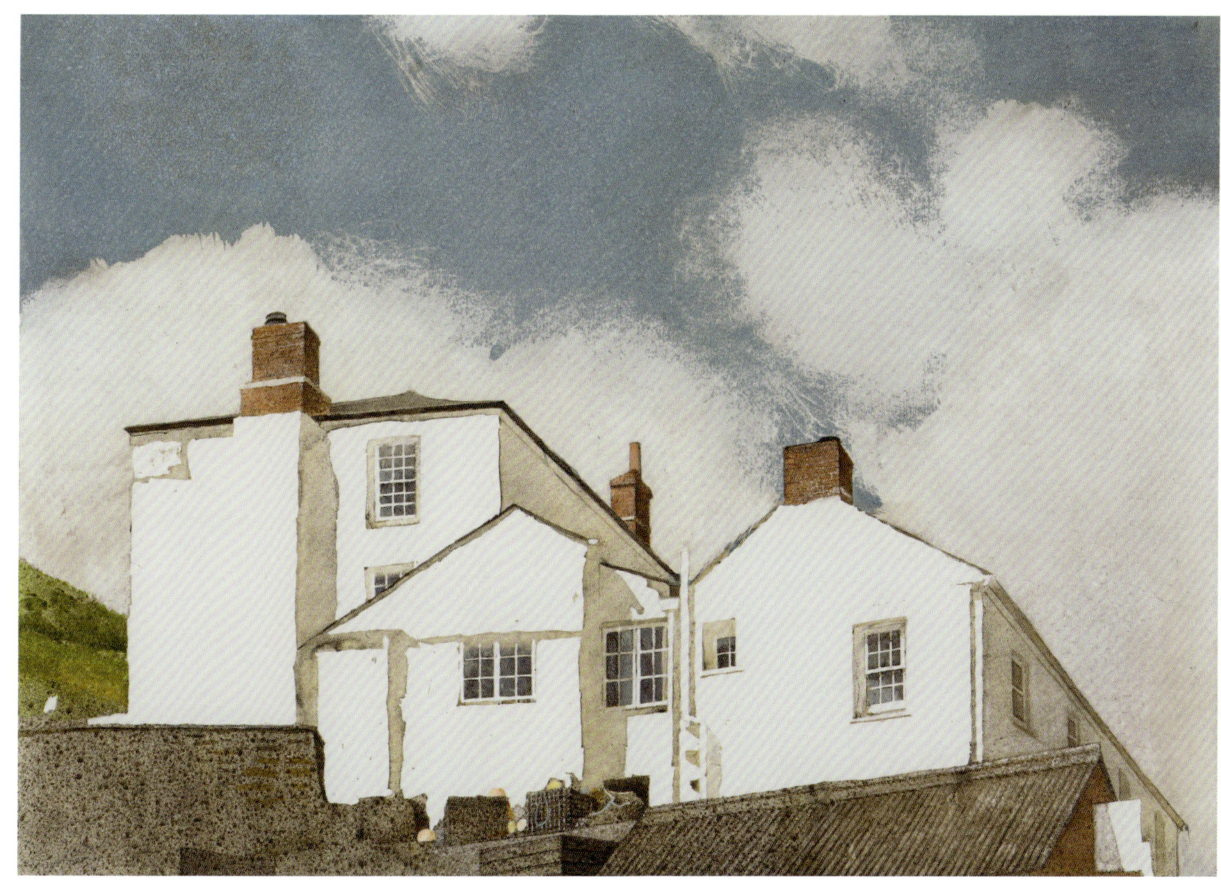

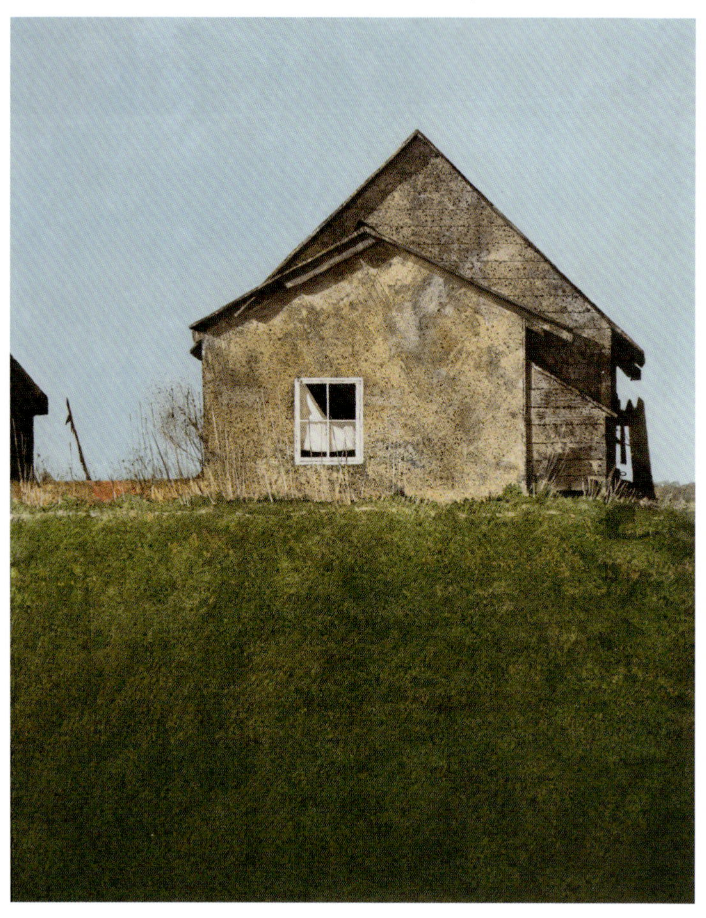

◂ 24 Fisherman's Hut, Southwold
acrylic on canvas on panel
79 x 61 cms 31 x 24 ins

▾ 25 Abandoned House behind Dry Stone Wall, Rawtenstall
acrylic on canvas on panel
64 x 55 cms 25¼ x 21⅝ ins

▸ 26 Quayside Boat, Morston II
acrylic on canvas on panel
94 x 72 cms 37 x 28⅜ ins

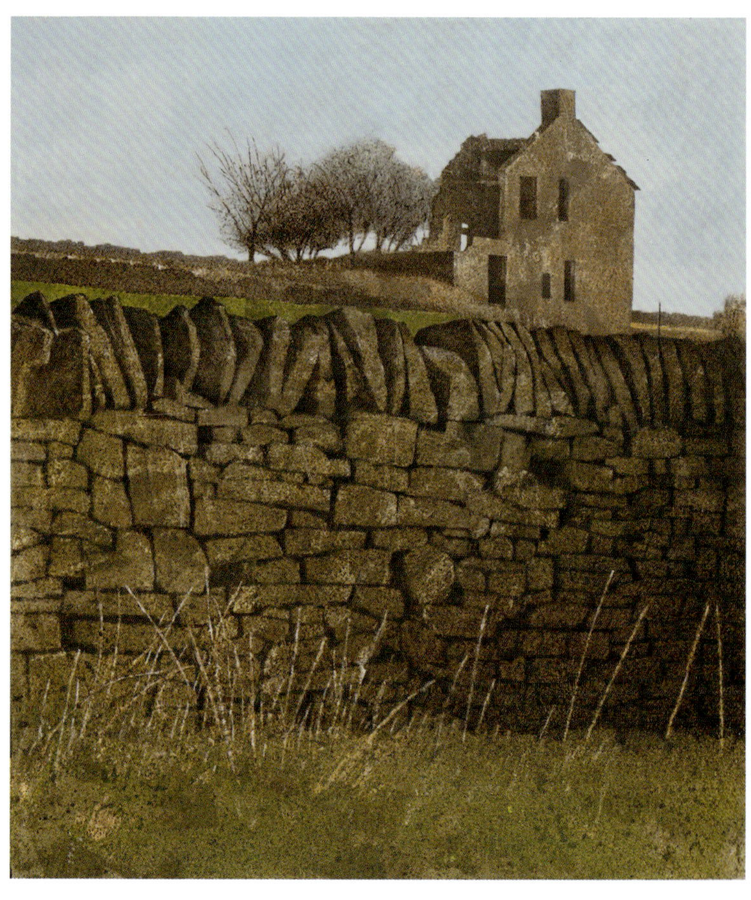

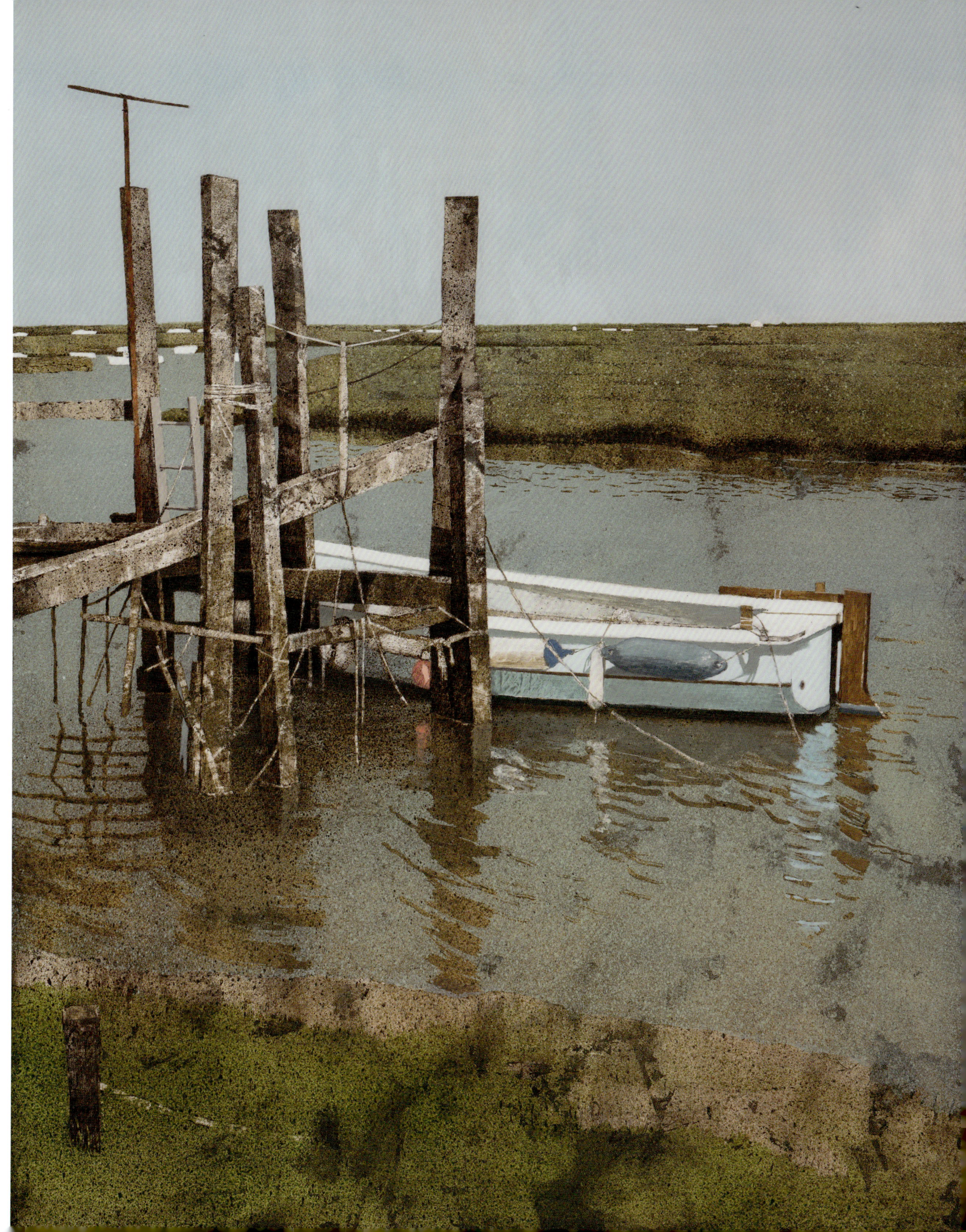

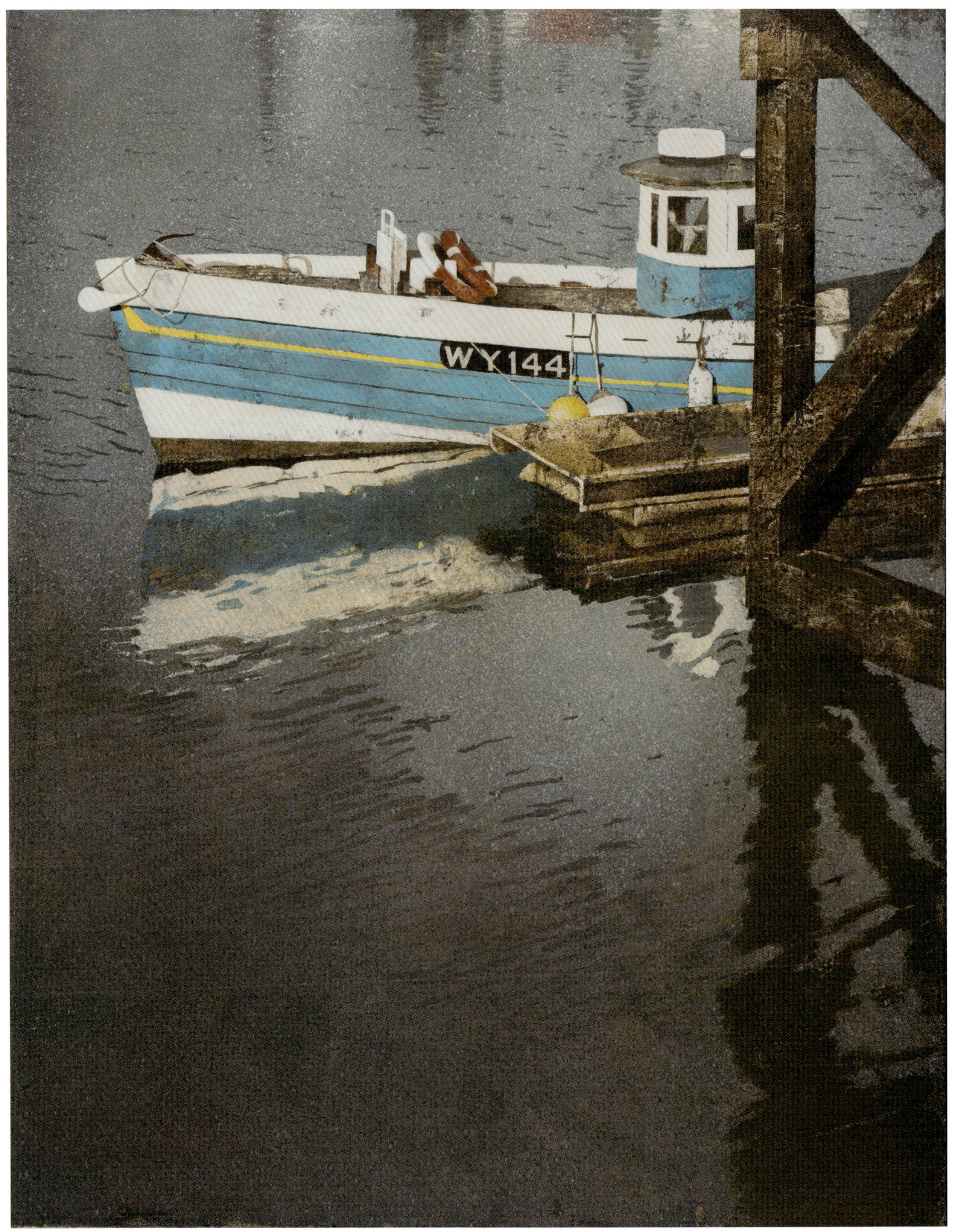
WY144

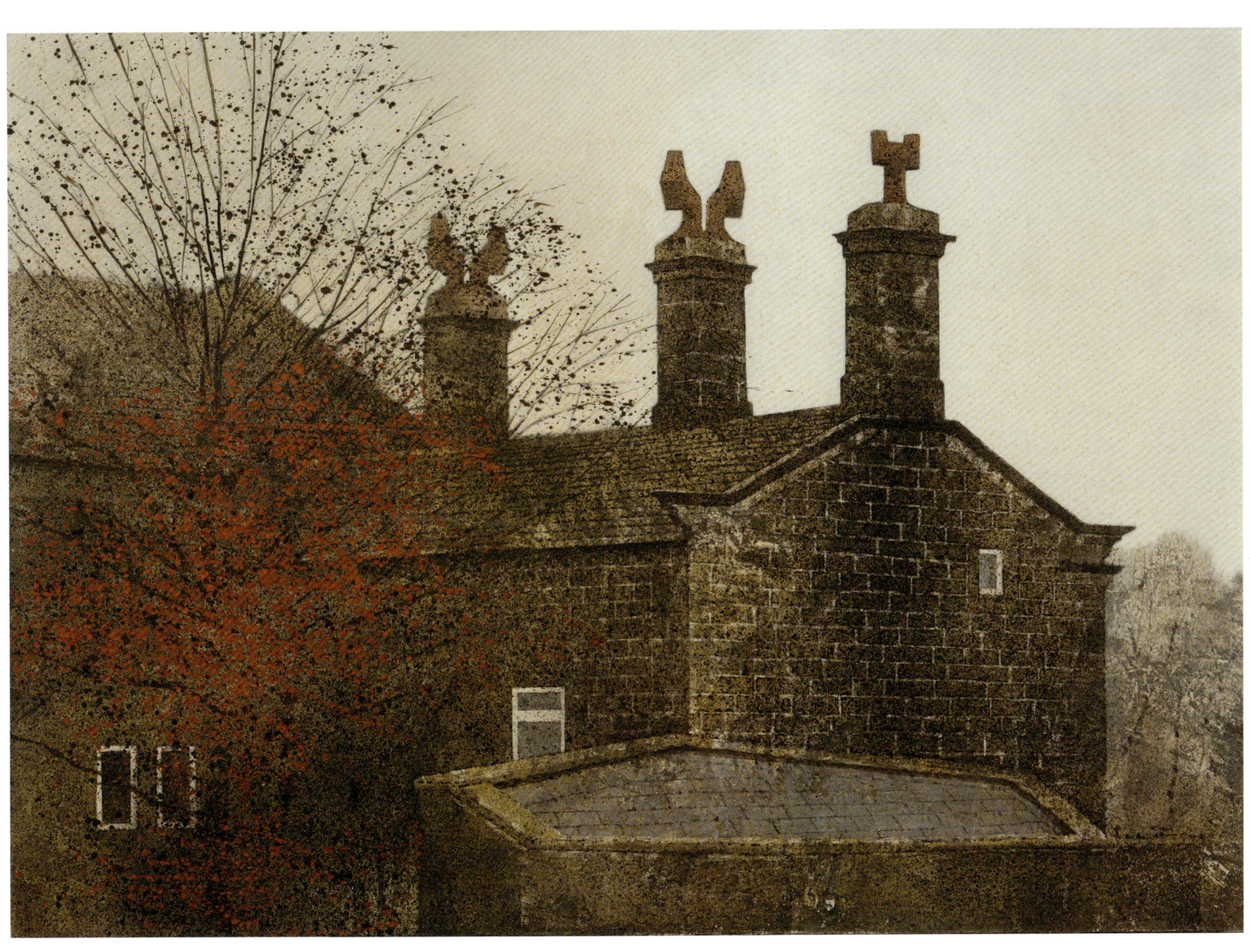

◂ 27 Fishing Vessel, Whitby
acrylic on canvas on panel
84 x 65 cms 33 x 25½ ins

▴ 28 Heptonstall House, Copper Beech, Autumn
acrylic on canvas on panel
55 x 74 cms 21½ x 29 ins

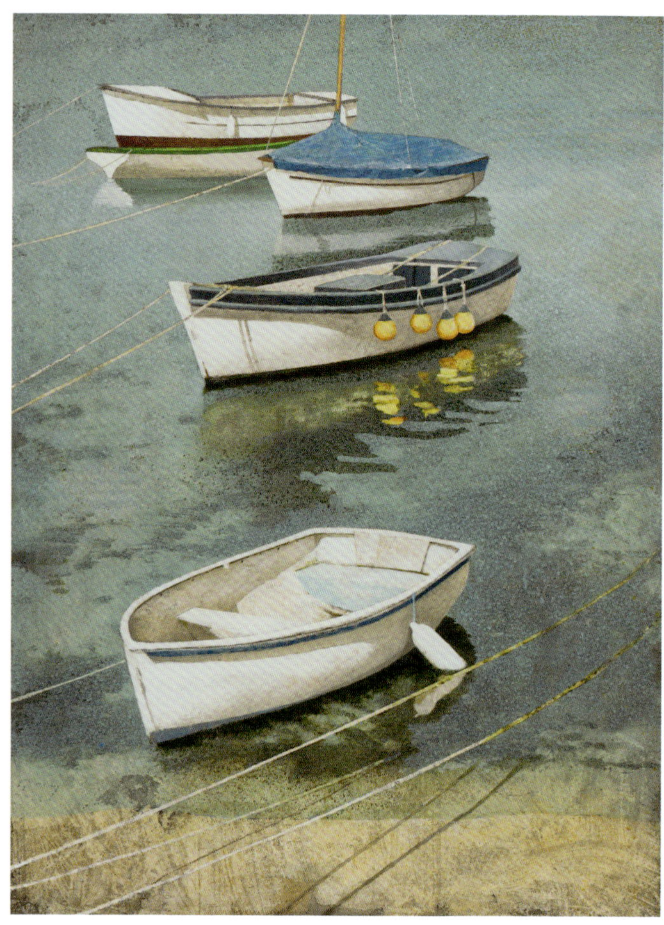

◀ 29 Mousehole Harbour Boats V
acrylic on canvas on panel
74 x 53 cms 29 x 21 ins

▼ 30 Coverack Harbour, Incoming Sea Fret
acrylic on canvas on panel
79 x 56 cms 31 x 22 ins

▶ 31 Blue Boats, Flushing
acrylic on canvas
53 x 69 cms 21 x 27 ins

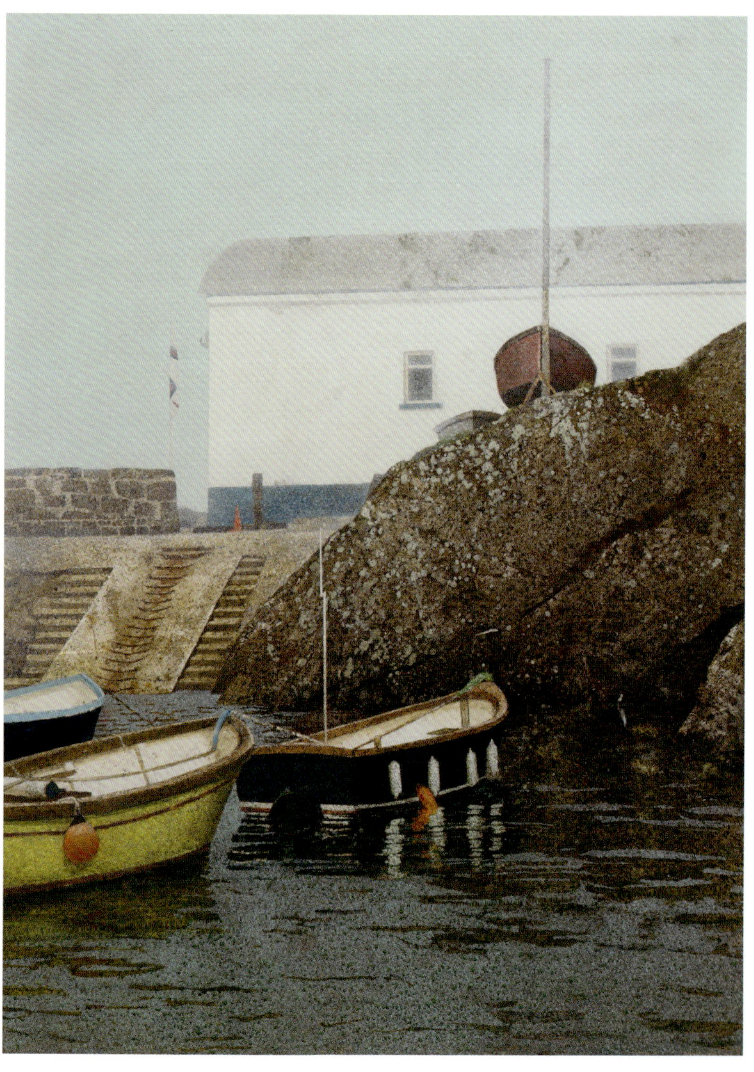

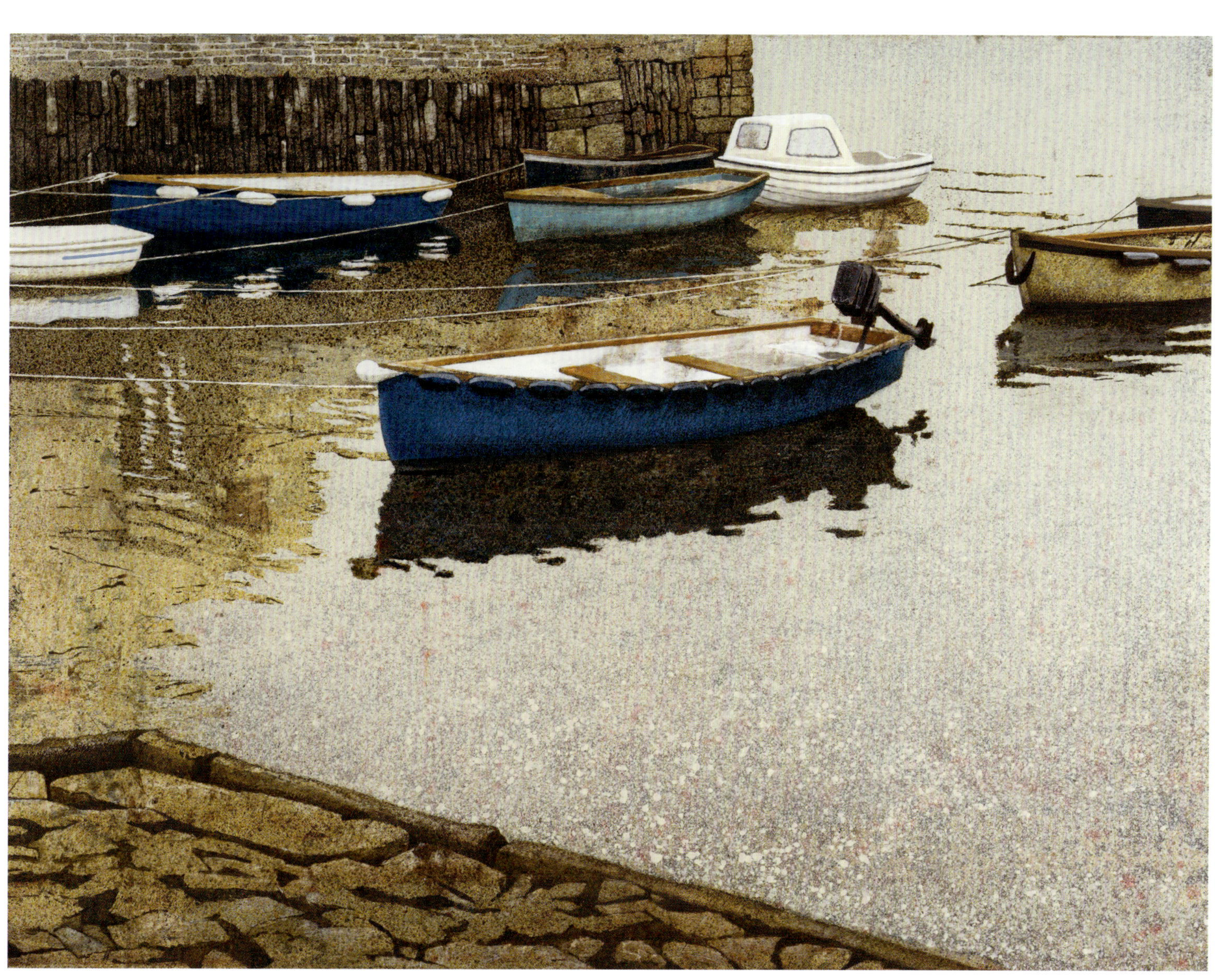

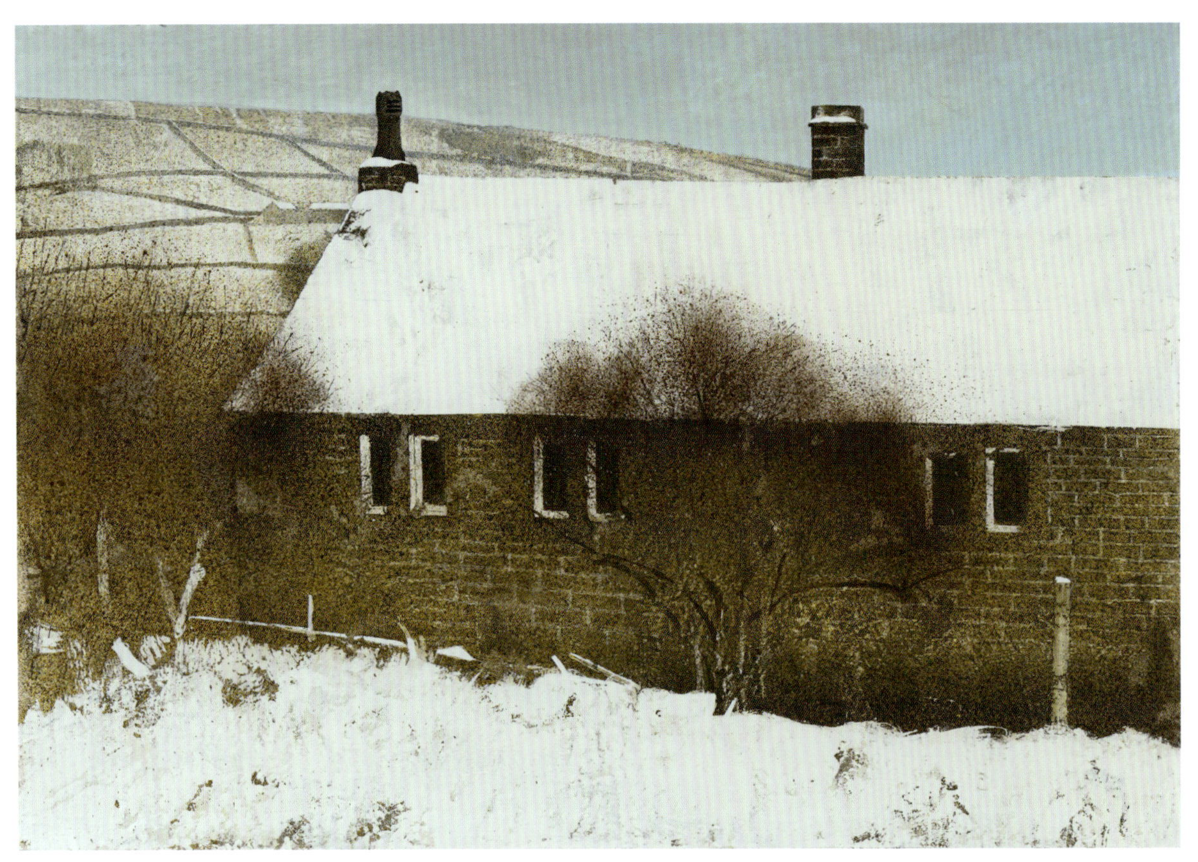

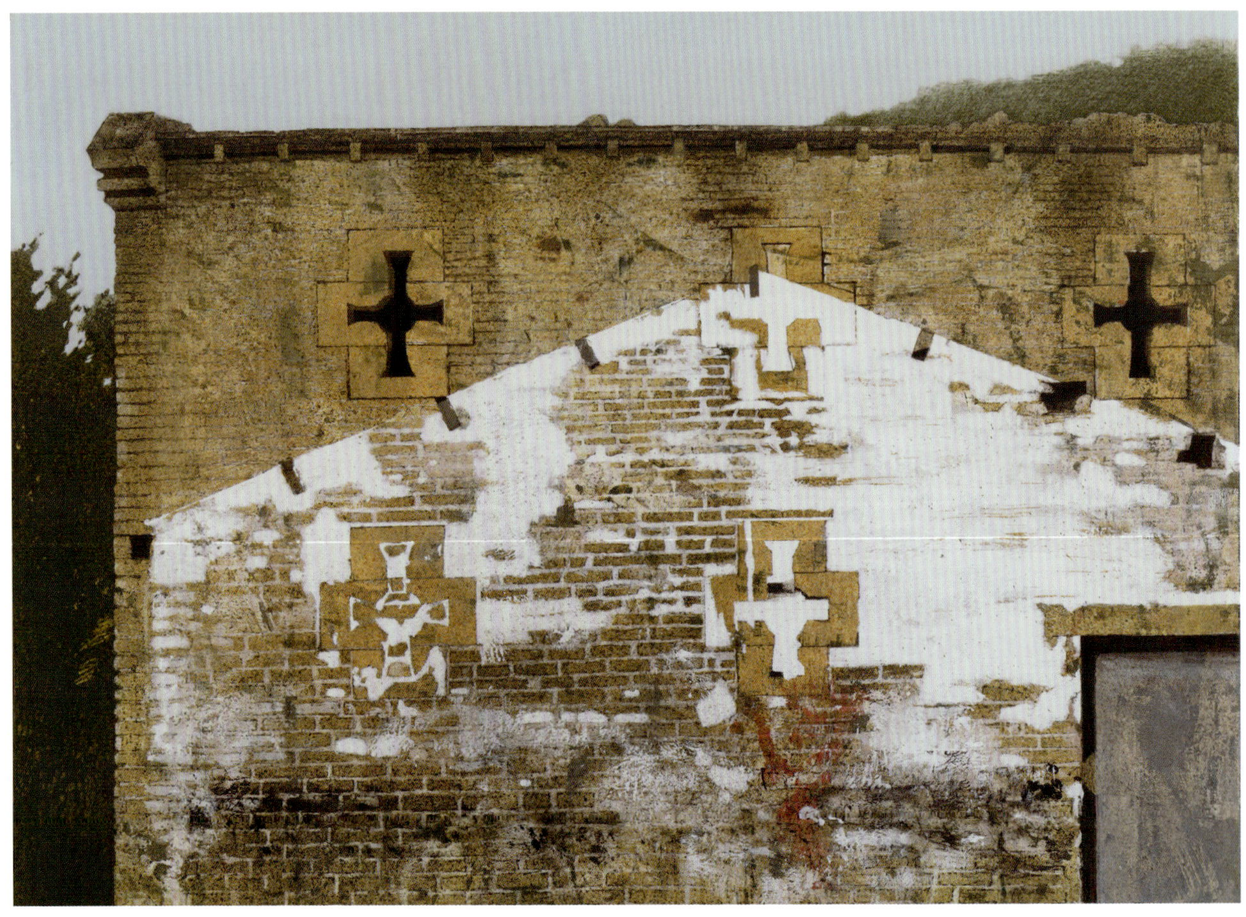

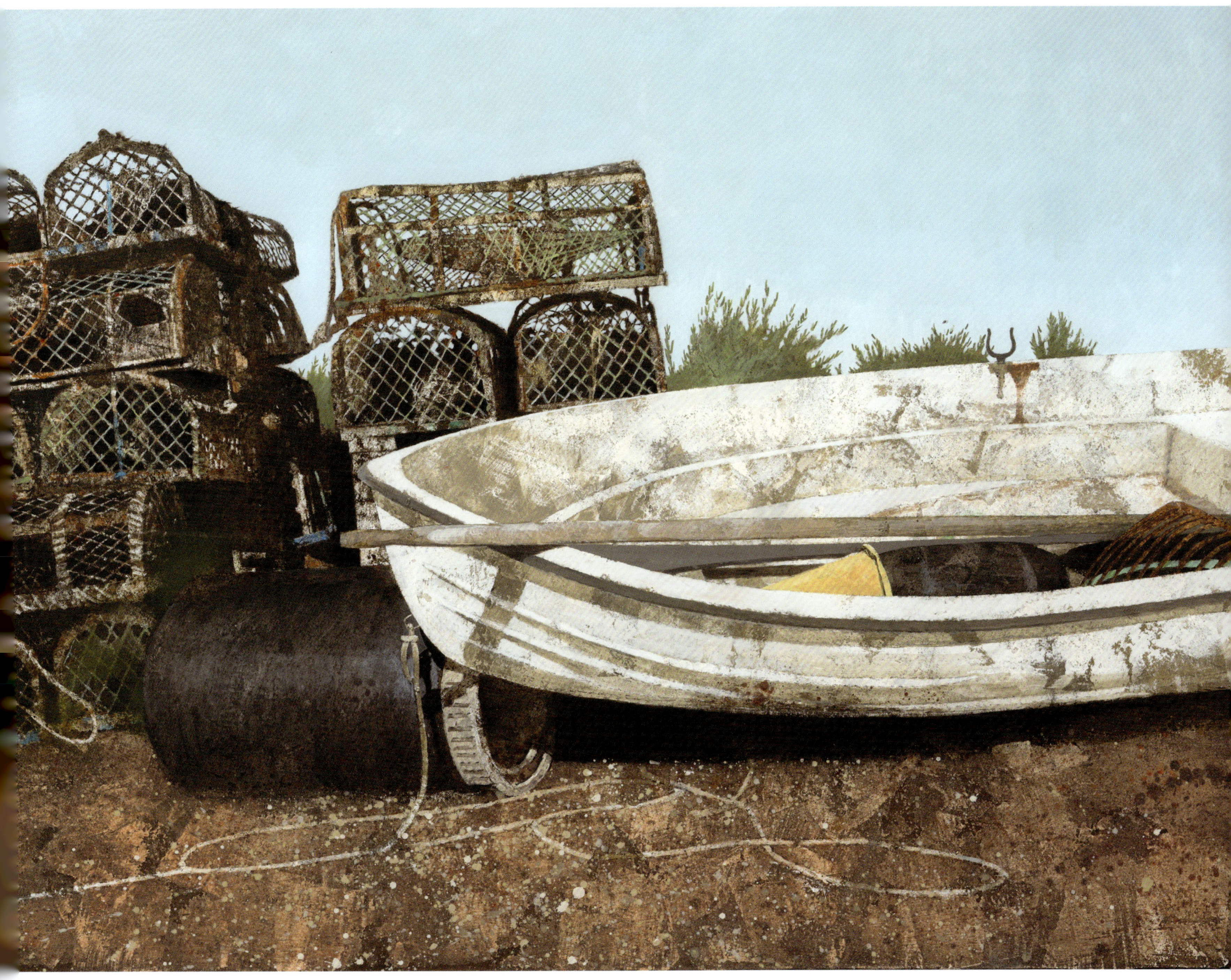

◤ 32 Abandoned House above Marsden, II
acrylic on canvas on panel
58 x 81 cms 23 x 32 ins

◀ 33 Barn Wall Palimpsest
acrylic on canvas on panel
61 x 84 cms 24 x 33 ins

▲ 34 Brancaster Staithe Harbour II
acrylic on canvas on panel
73 x 101 cms 28¾ x 39¾ ins

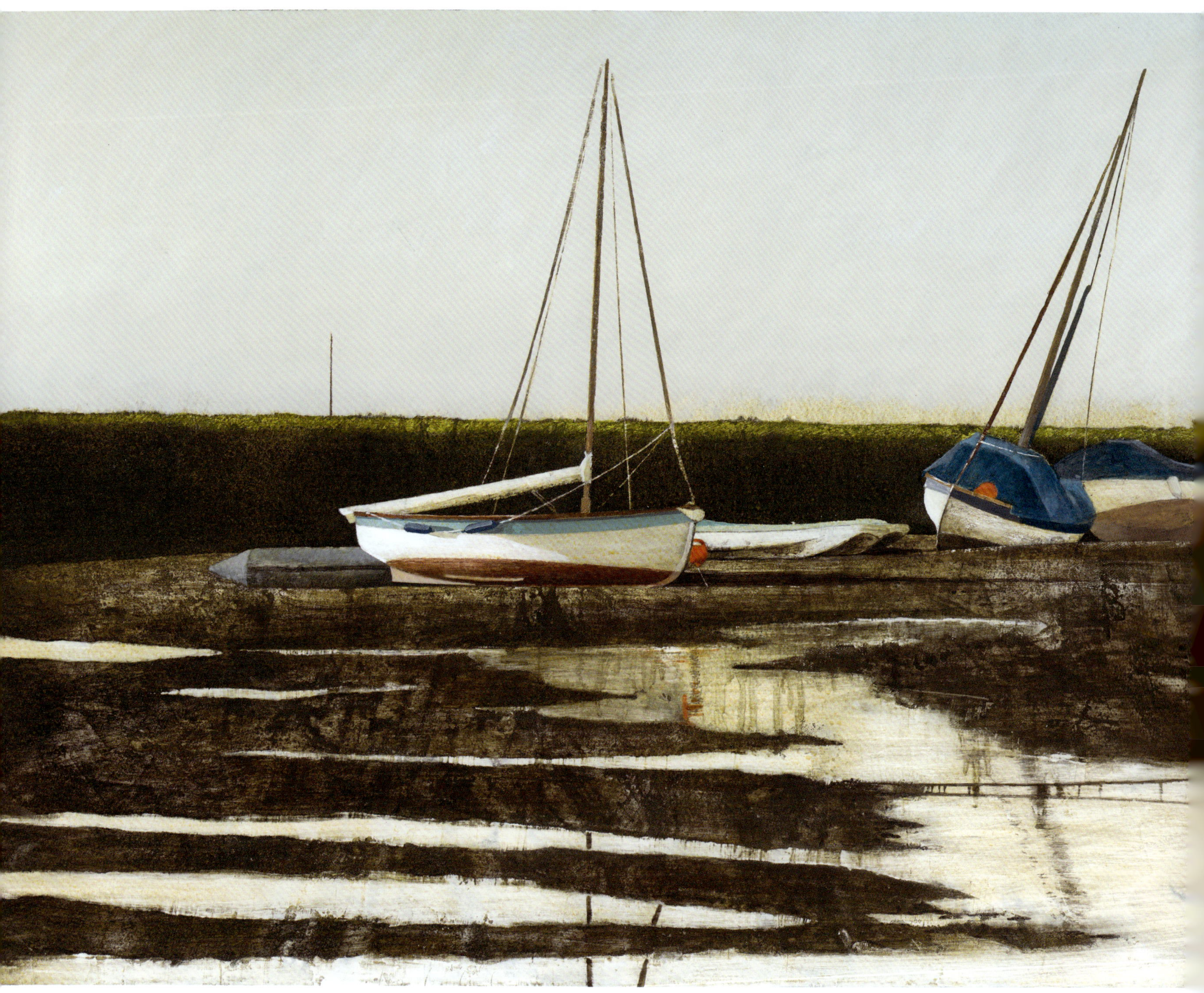

▲ 35 Lowtide Boats at Brancaster Staithe, Late Afternoon II
acrylic on canvas
61 x 77 cms 24 x 30½ ins

▶ 36 Quayside near Blakeney
acrylic on paper
64 x 52 cms 25¼ x 20½ ins

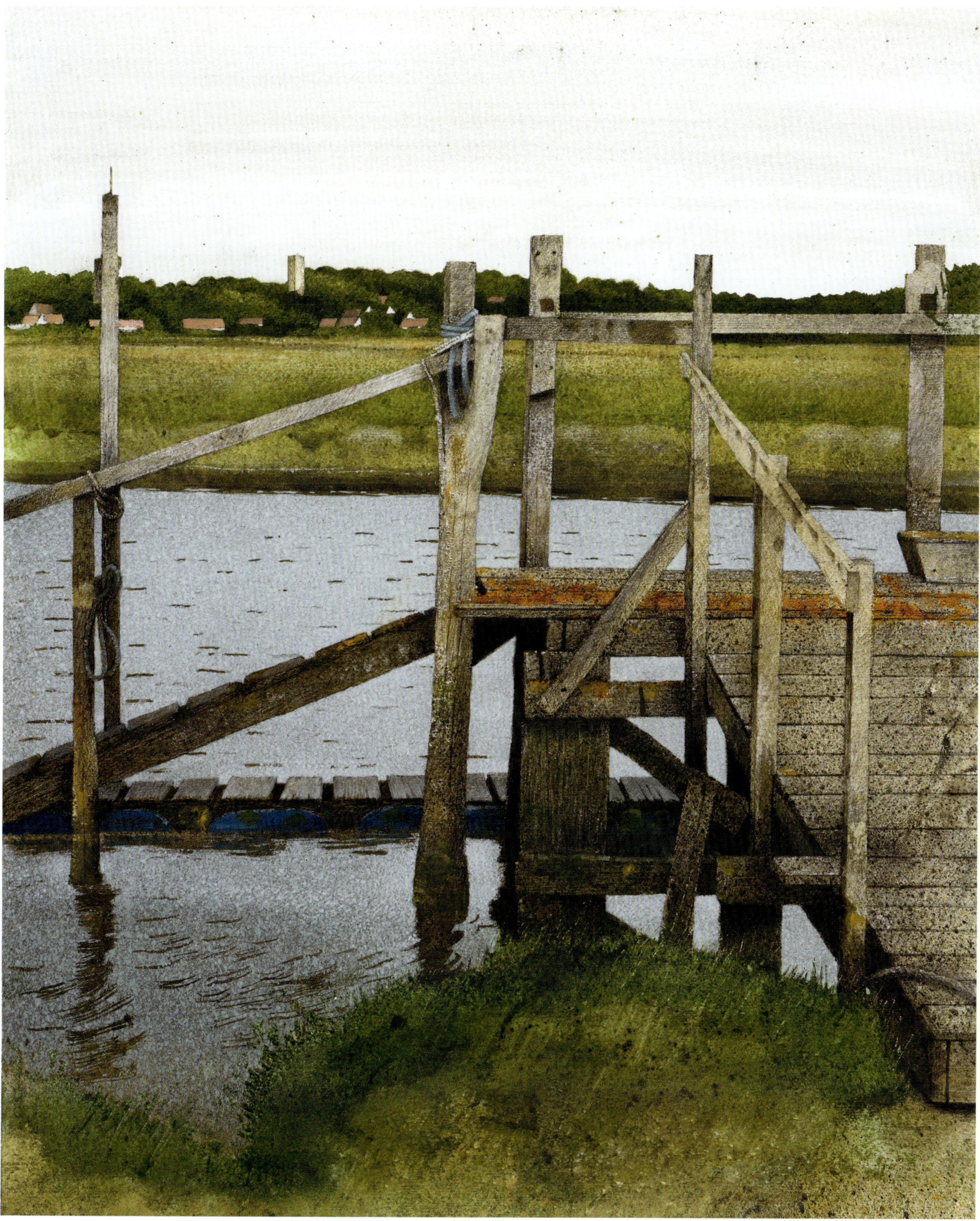

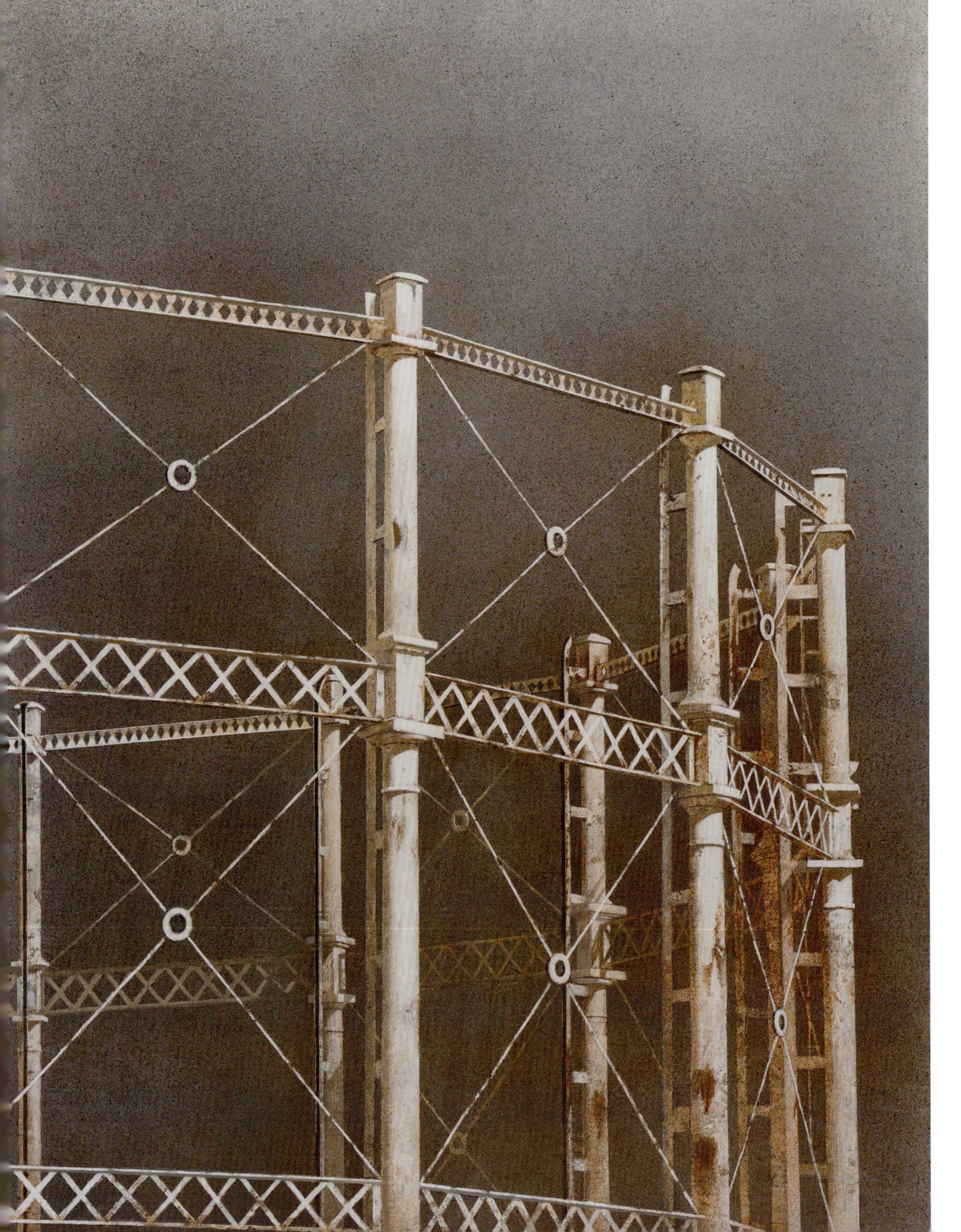

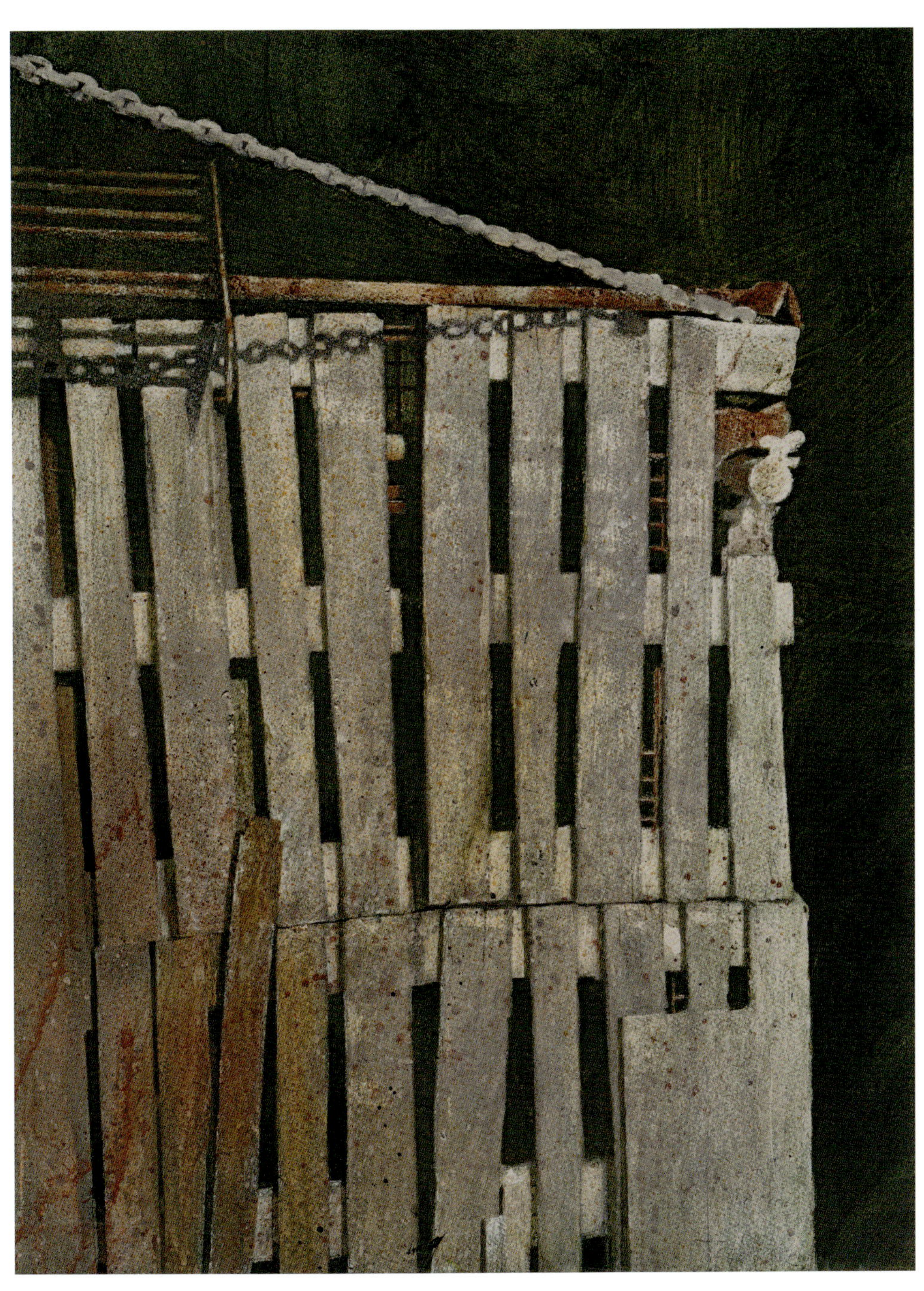

◀ 37 Gasometer II
acrylic on canvas on panel
122 x 90 cms 48 x 35⅜ ins

▲ 38 Jetty, 2014
acrylic on Velin Arches cream paper
72 x 52 cms 28⅜ x 20½ ins

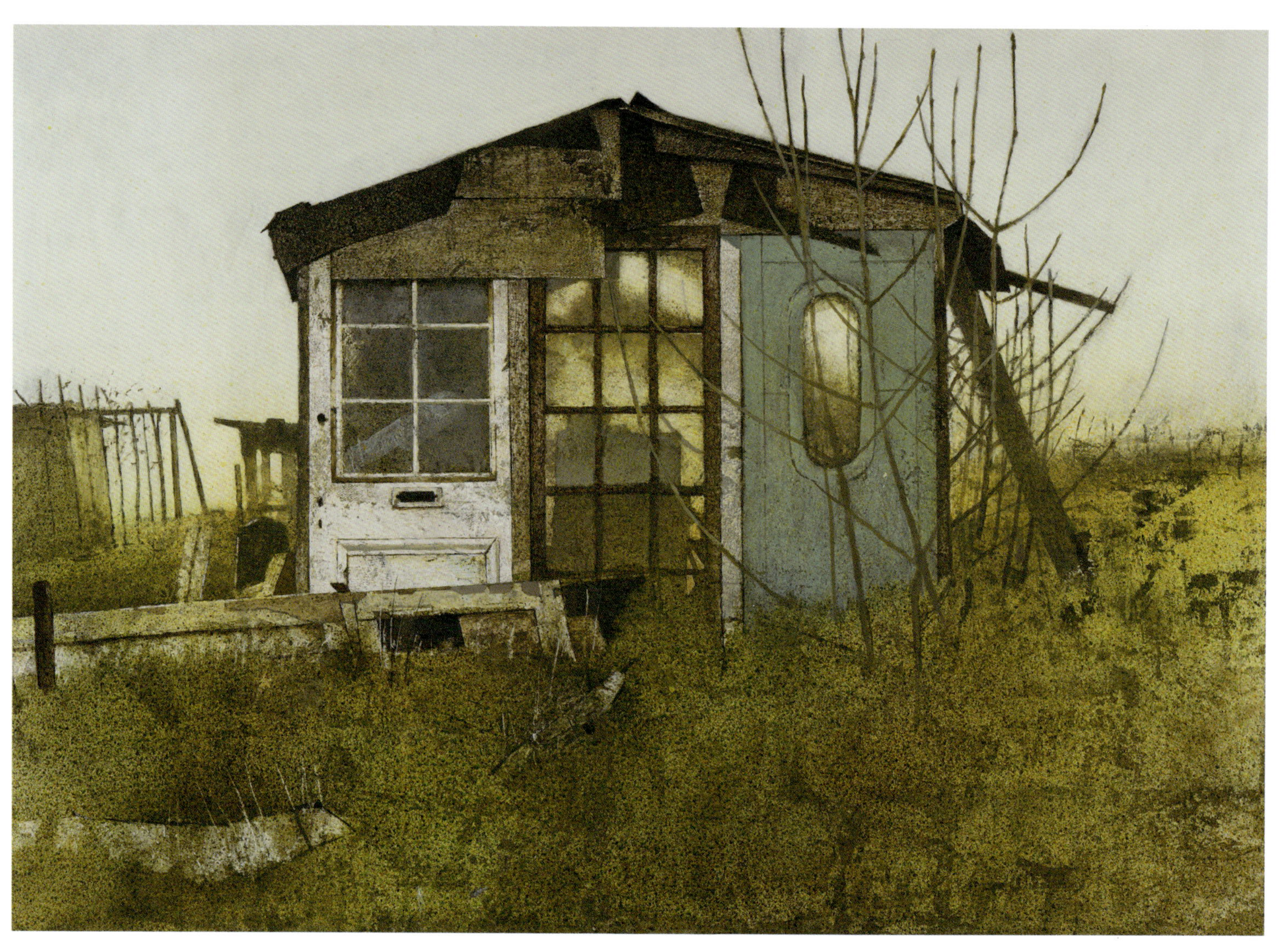

39 Allotment Shed
acrylic on canvas on panel
53 x 74 cms 21 x 29 ins

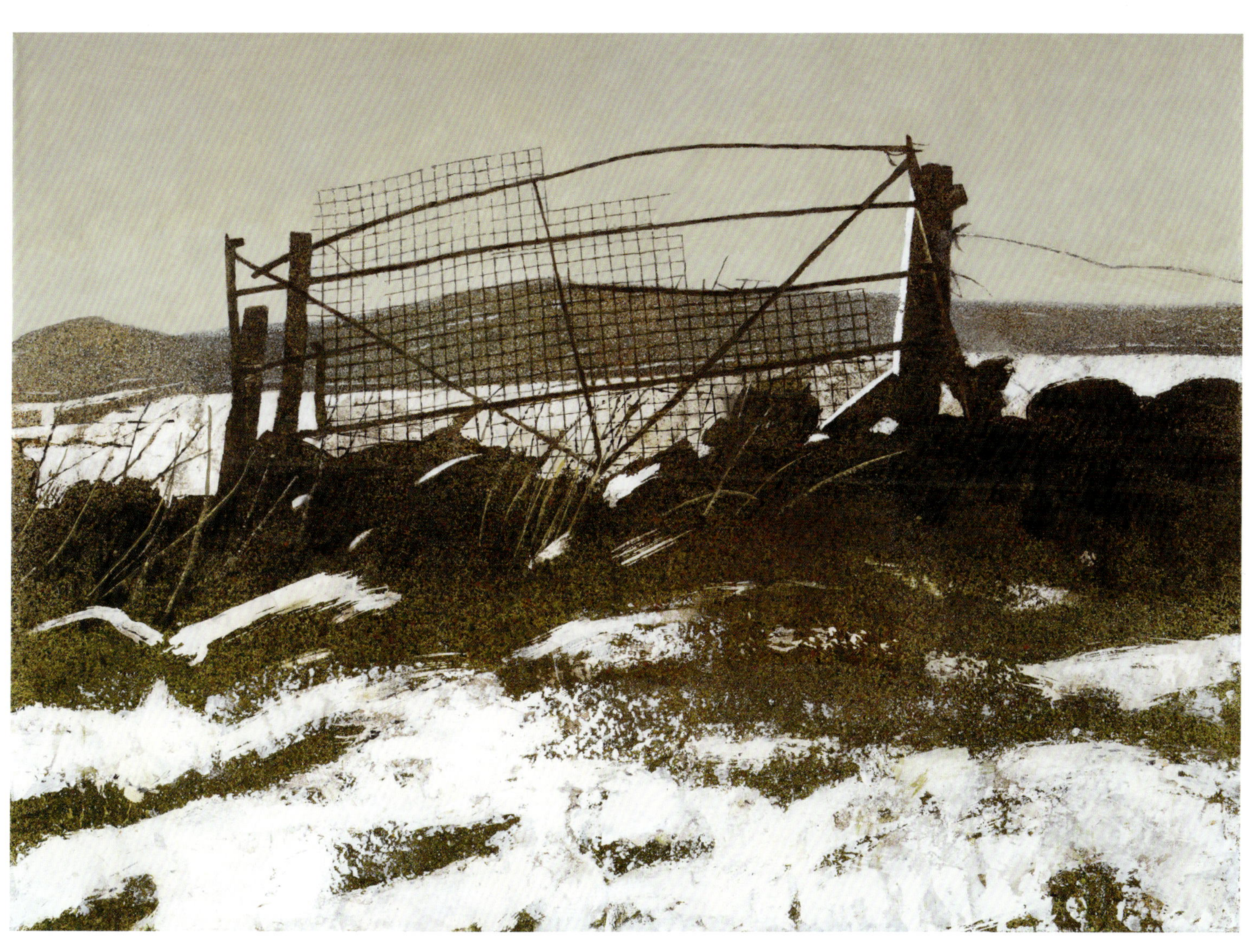

40 Moorland Gate With Snow
acrylic on canvas on panel
55 x 74 cms 21½ x 29 ins

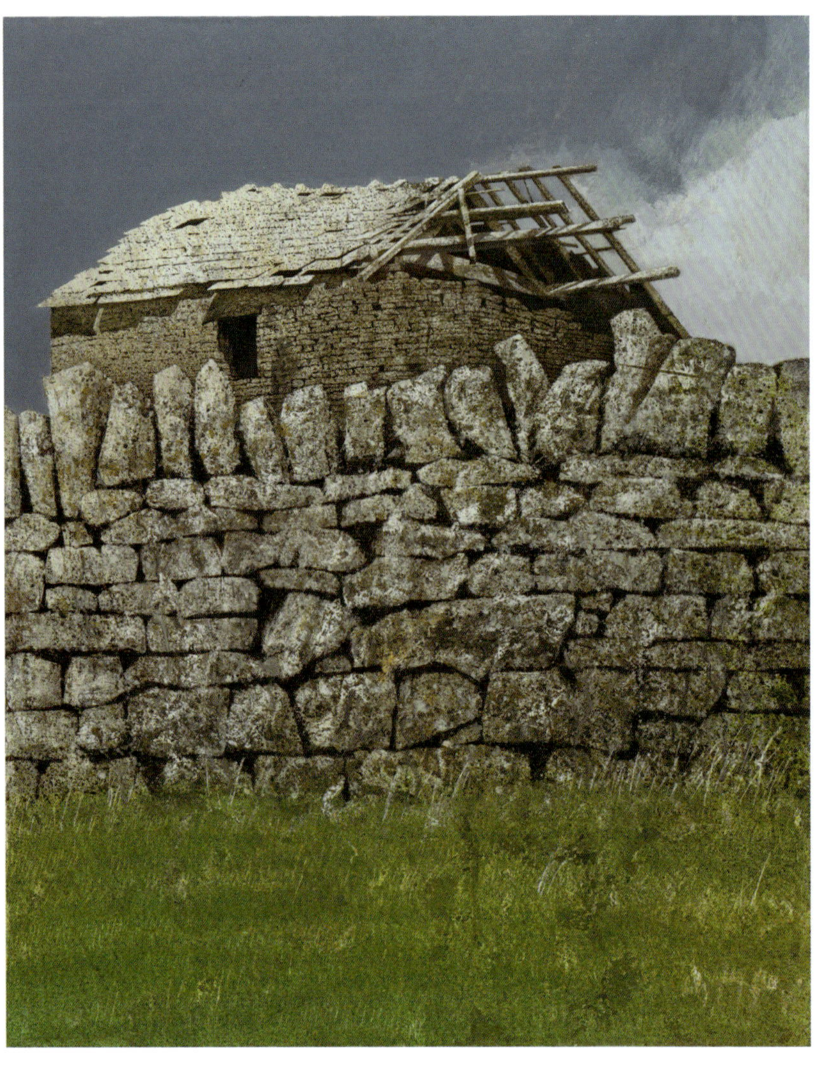

◀ 41 Abandoned Farm with Drystone Wall, North Pennines
acrylic on canvas on panel
77 x 61 cms 30½ x 24 ins

▼ 42 Abandoned Farm, North Pennines, Late Spring
acrylic on canvas on panel
53 x 74 cms 21 x 29 ins

▶ 43 Lighthouse with Morning Shadows, Flamborough Head I
acrylic on canvas on panel
75 x 61 cms 29½ x 24 ins

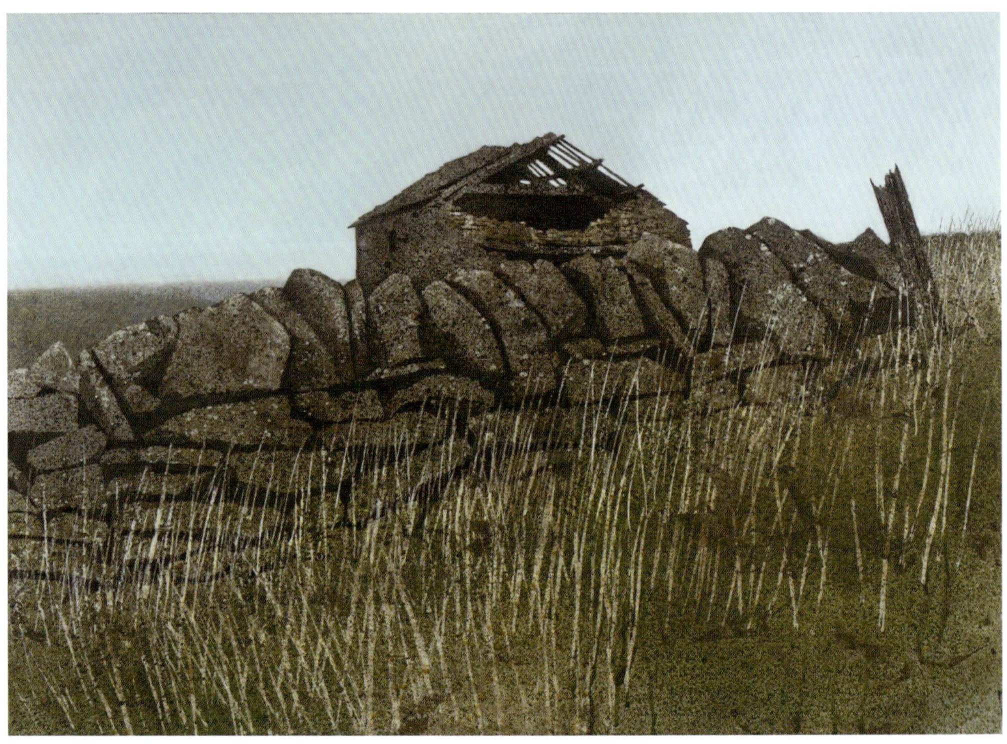

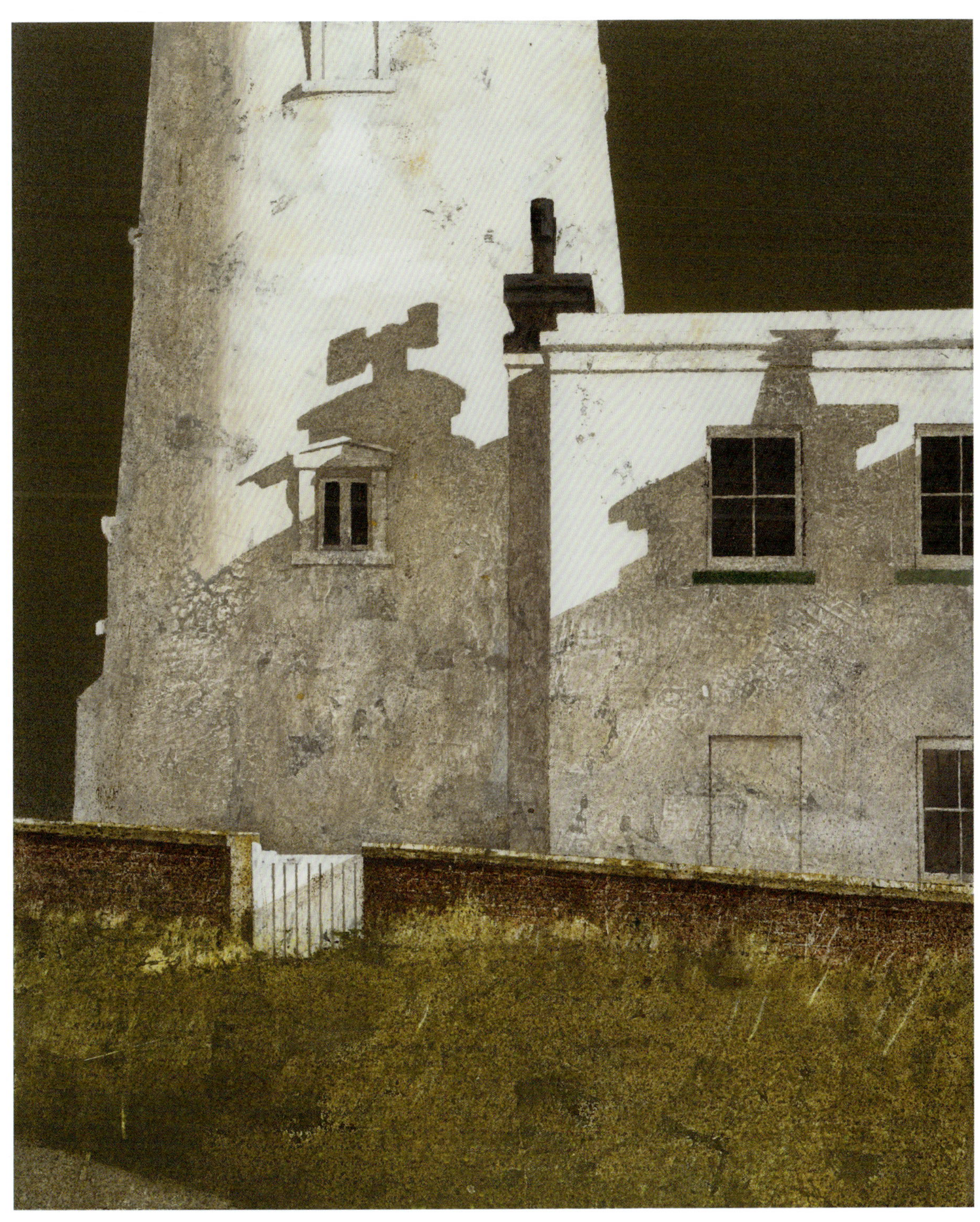

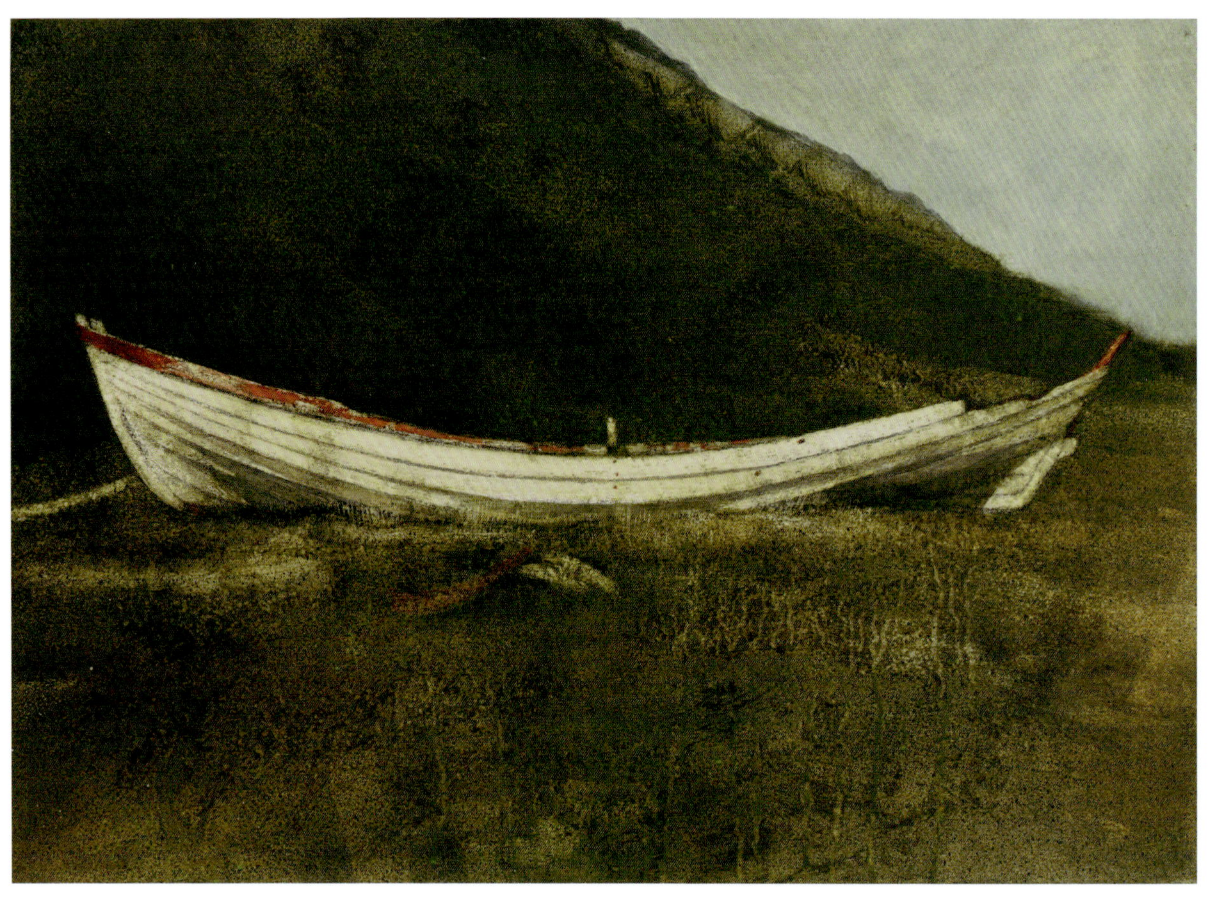

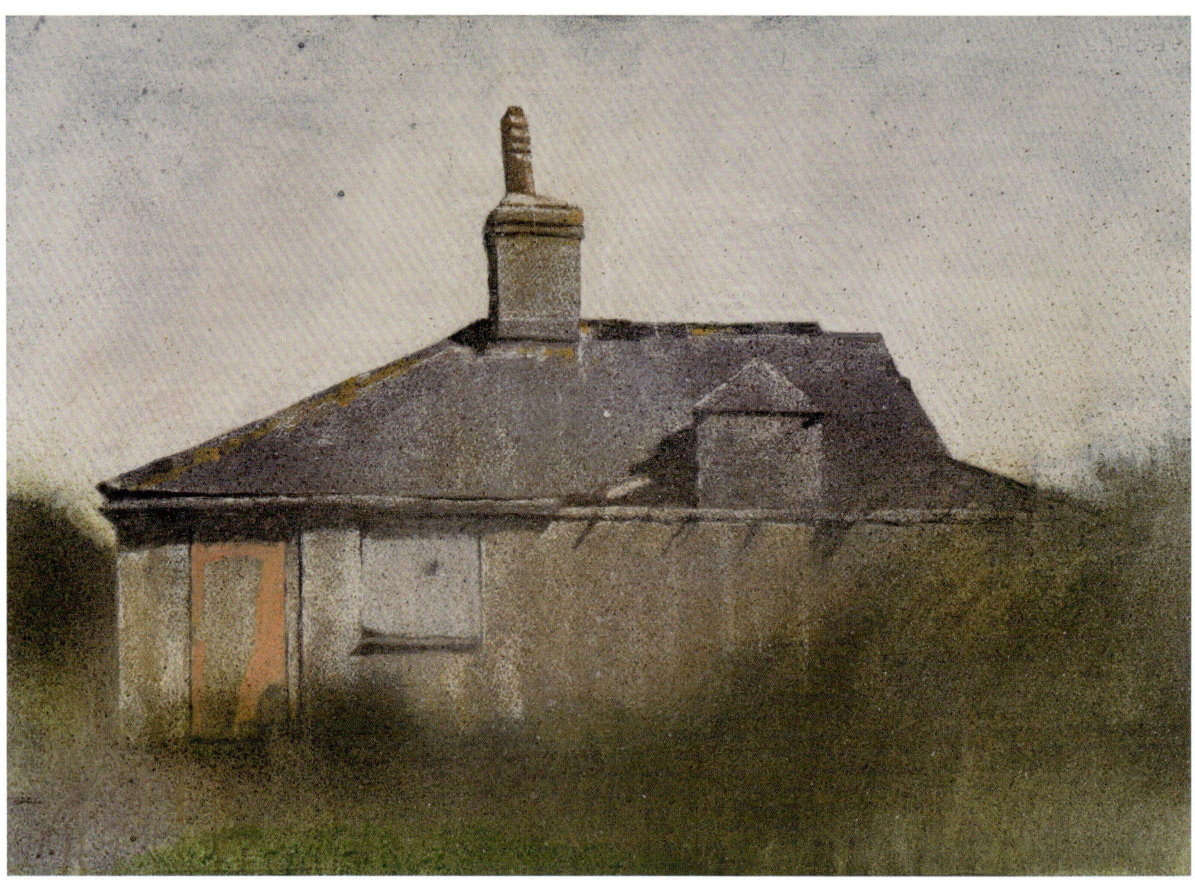

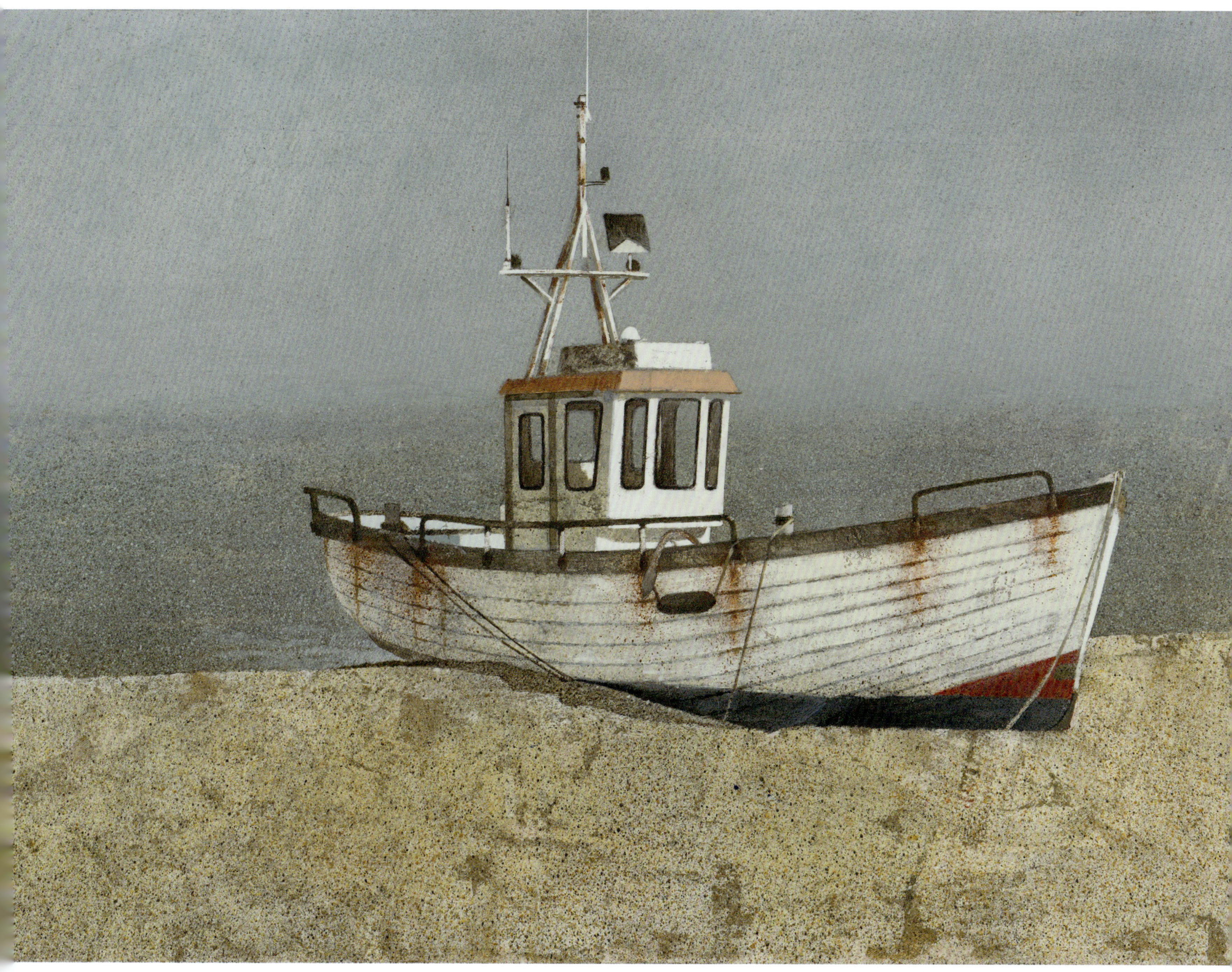

◤ 44 Yorkshire Coble, Port Mulgrave I, 2015
acrylic on Velin Arches cream paper
53 x 73 cms 20⅞ x 28¾ ins

◀ 45 Abandoned House
acrylic on Velin Arches cream paper
54 x 73 cms 21¼ x 28¾ ins

▲ 46 Fishing Boat, Dungeness
acrylic on canvas on panel
61 x 83 cms 24 x 32½ ins

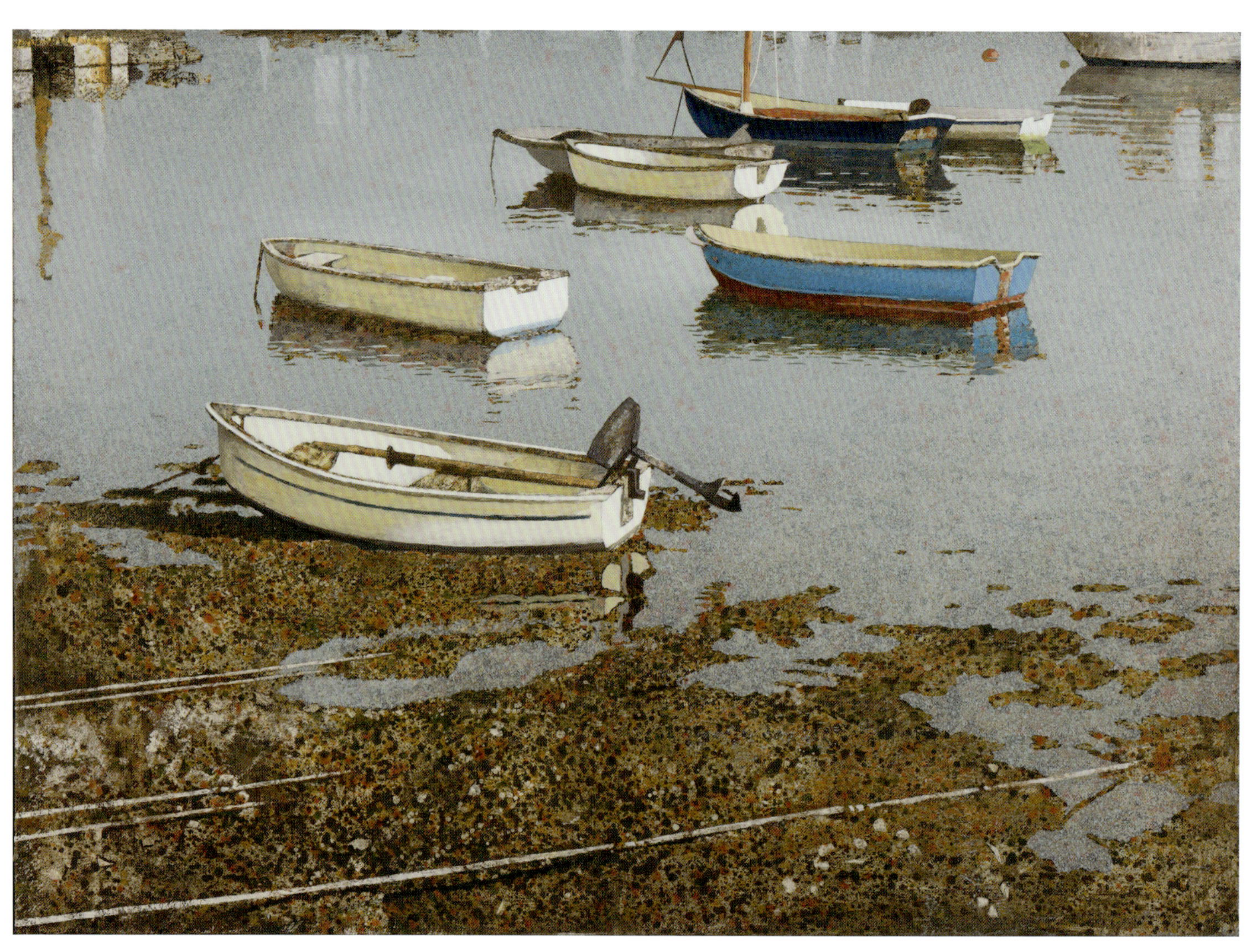

47 Boats, Incoming Tide, Percuil River II
acrylic on canvas
61 x 83 cms 24 x 32½ ins

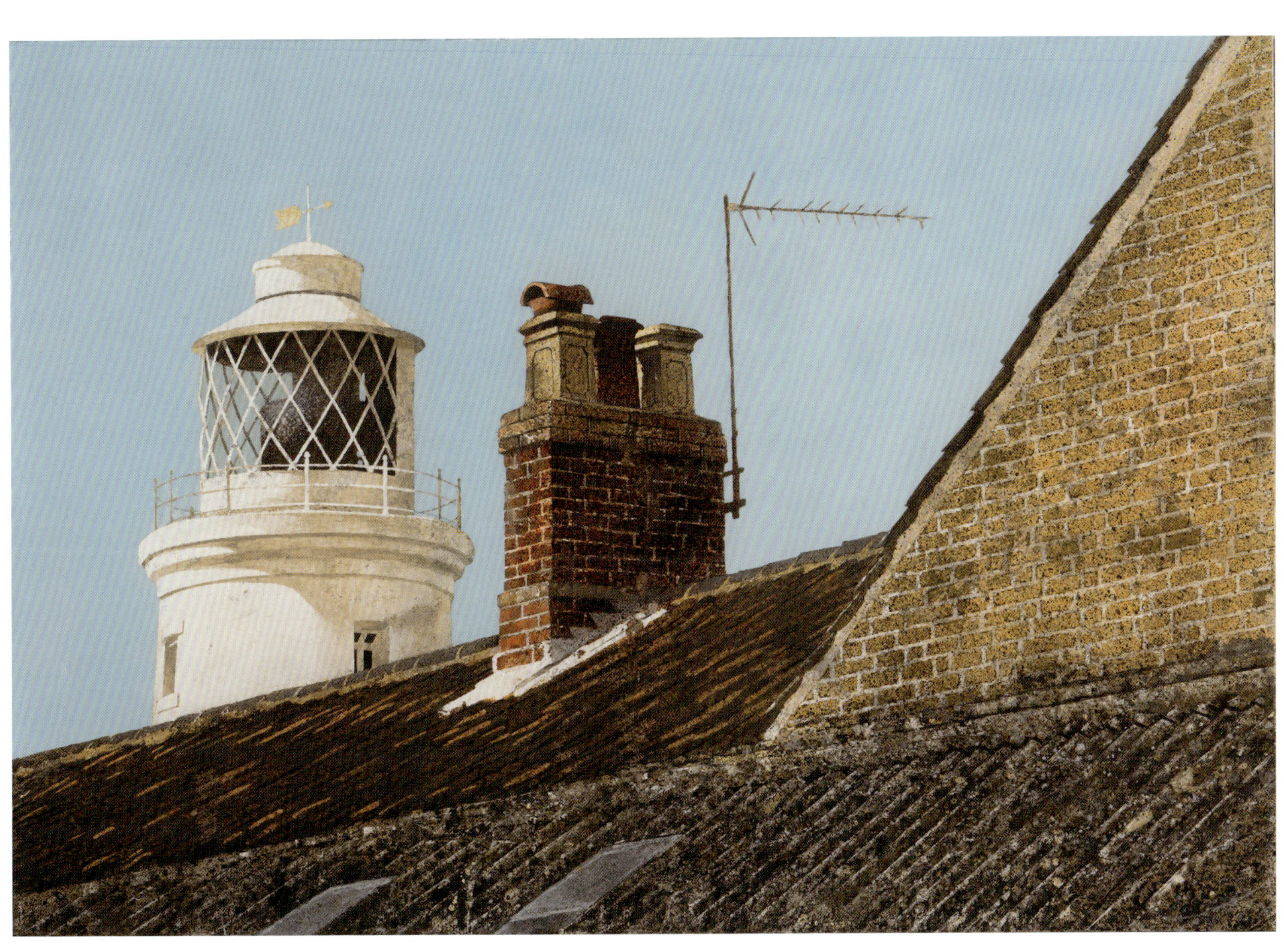

48 Southwold Rooftops I
acrylic on canvas on panel
61 x 86 cms 24 x 33⅞ ins

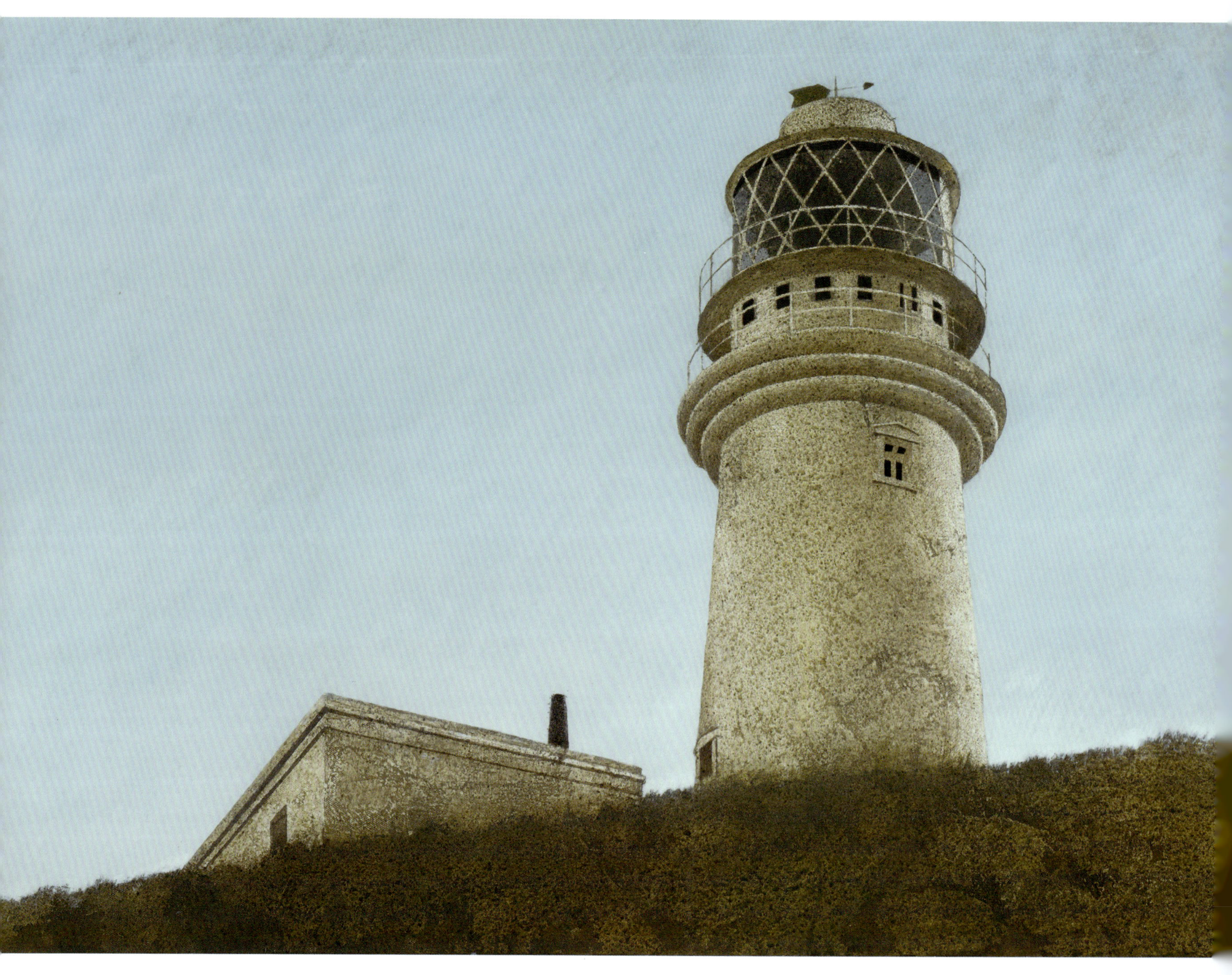

49 Late Afternoon, Flamborough Head Lighthouse
acrylic on canvas on panel
61 x 83 cms 24 x 32½ ins

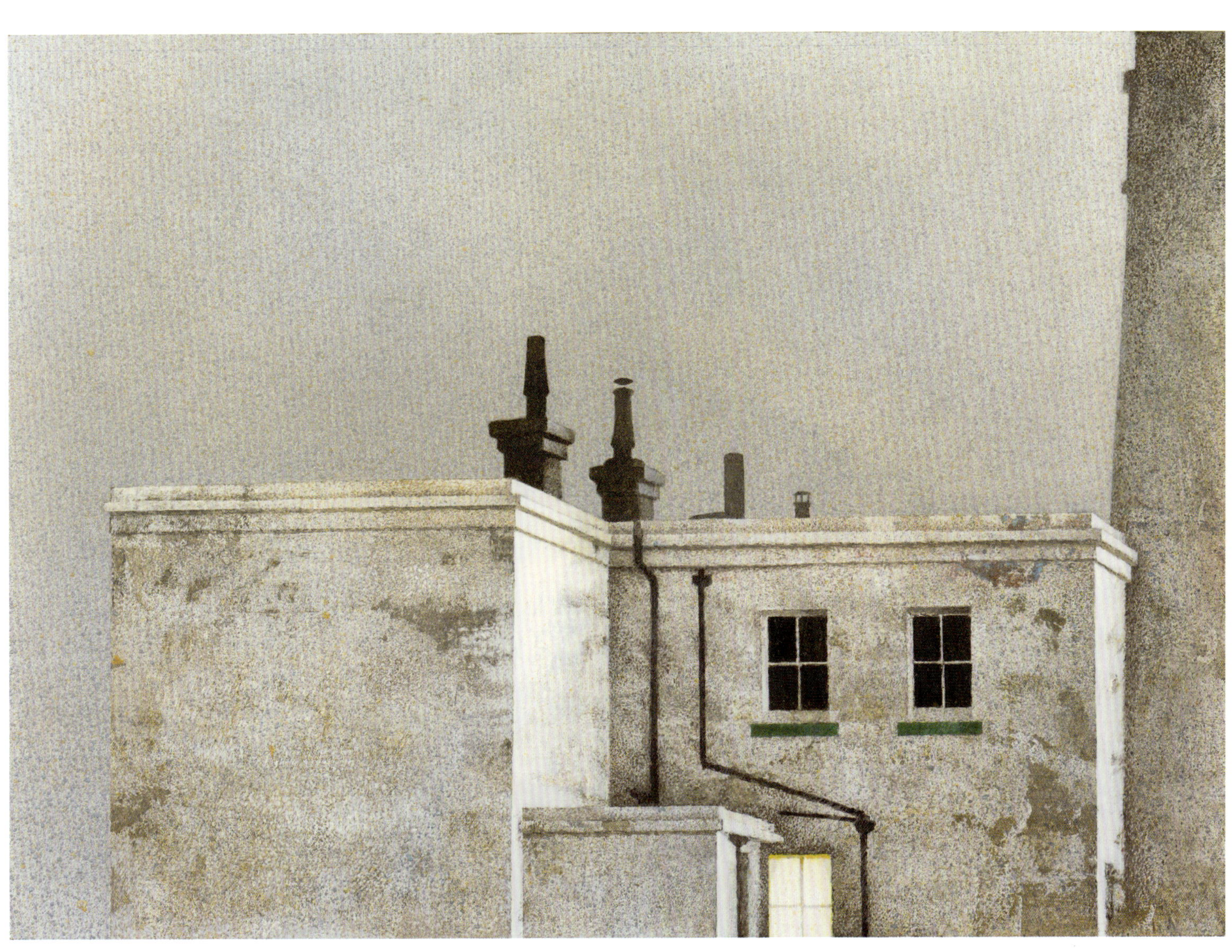

50 Dusk, Lighthouse, Flamborough
acrylic on canvas on panel
54 x 74 cms 21¼ x 29⅛ ins

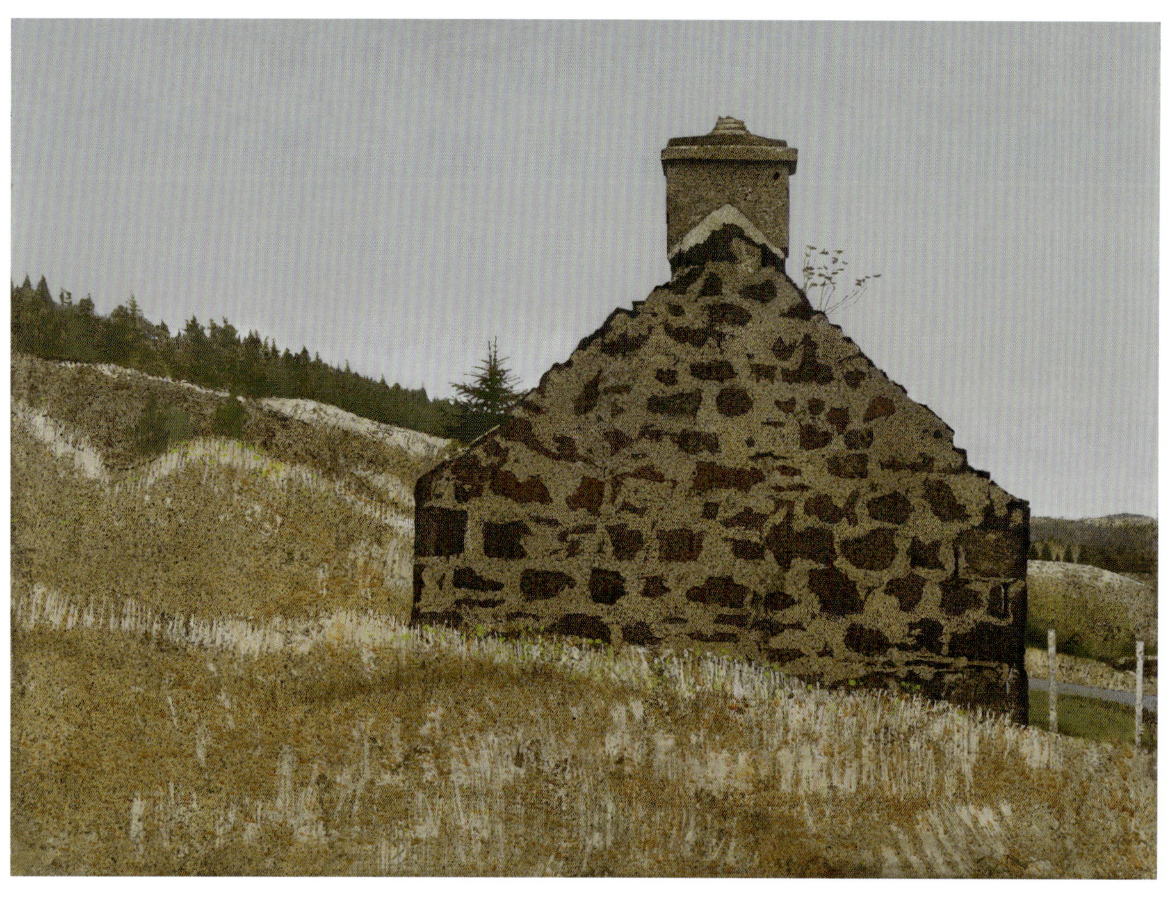

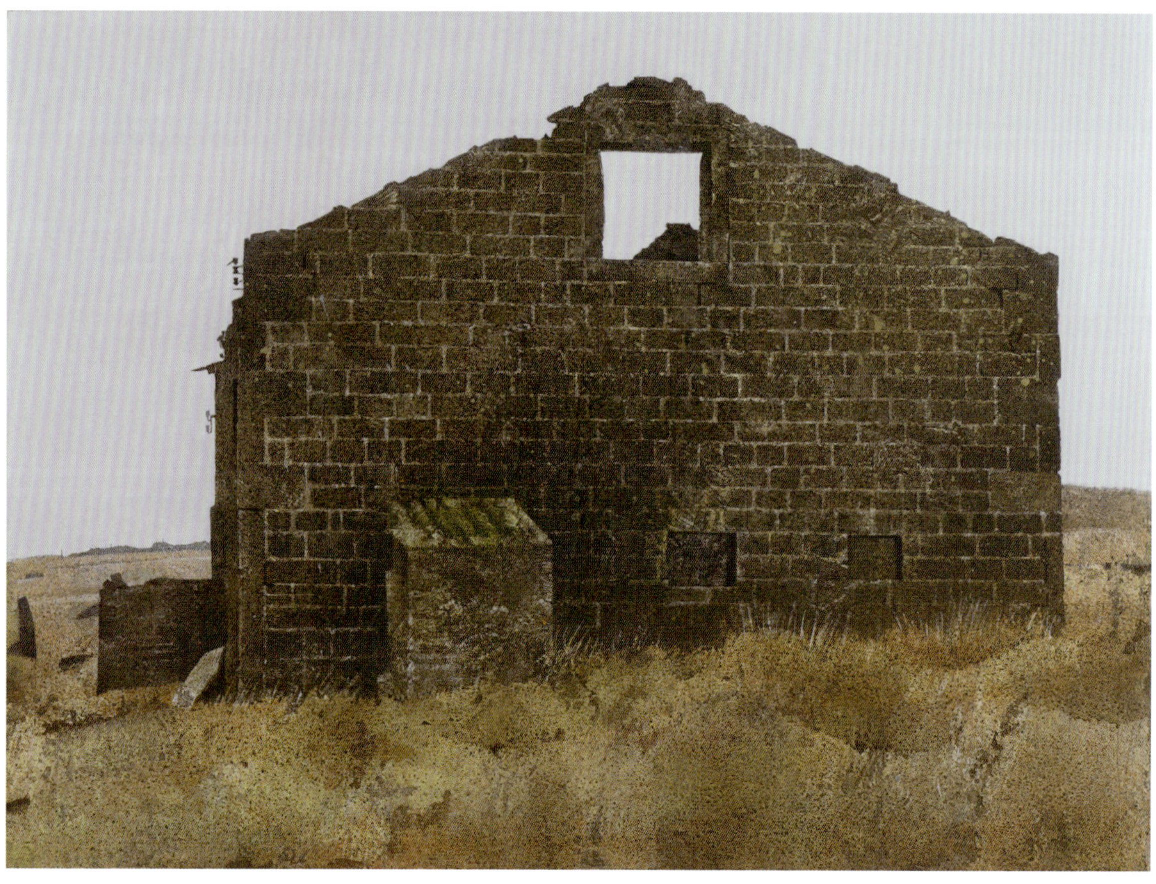

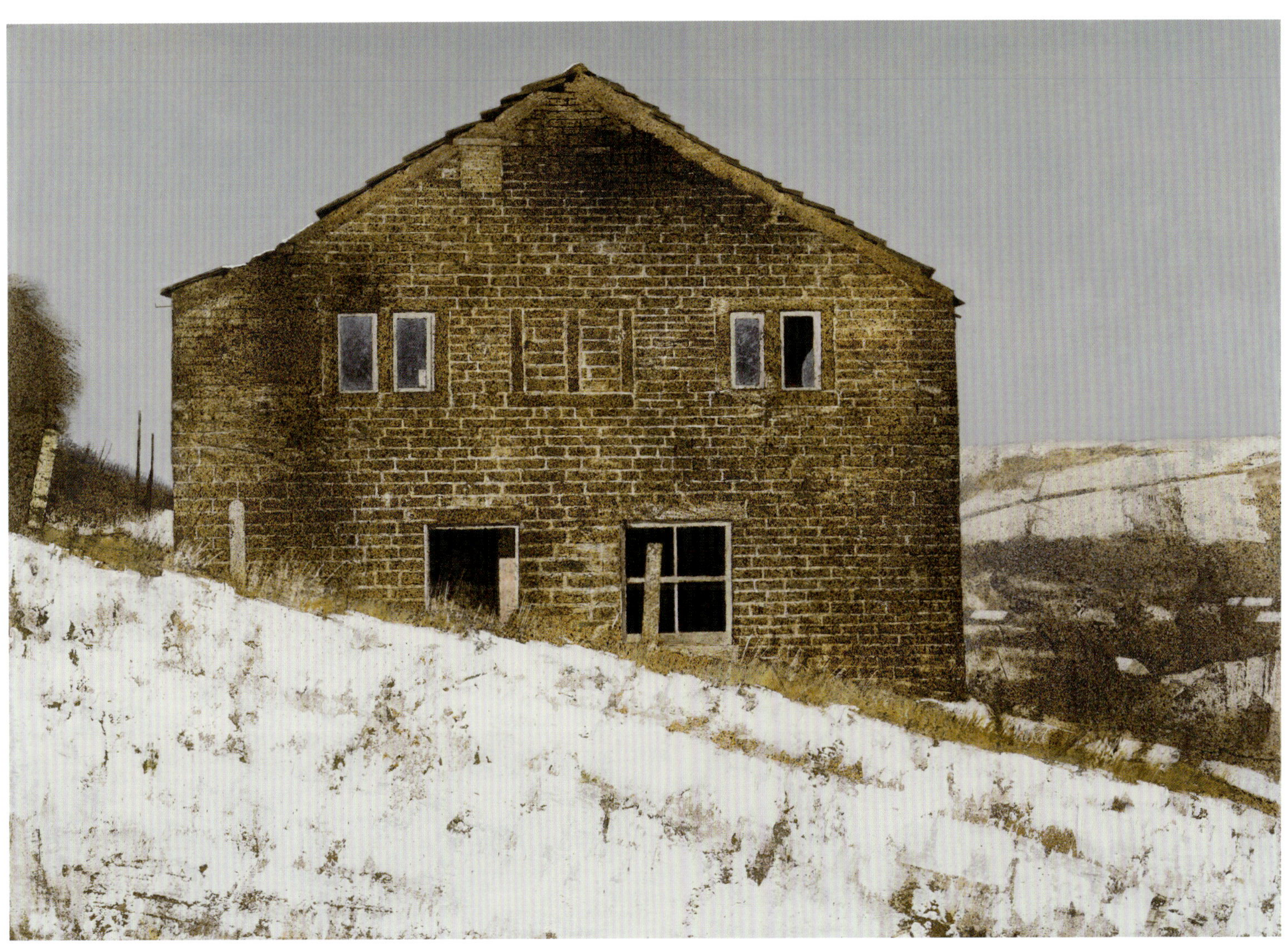

◤ 51 Abandoned Croft, Isle of Mull
acrylic on canvas on panel
65 x 86 cms 25½ x 34 ins

◀ 52 Moorland Gable End
acrylic on canvas on panel
66 x 86 cms 26 x 34 ins

▲ 53 Abandoned House Above Marsden
acrylic on canvas on panel
66 x 92 cms 26 x 36 ins

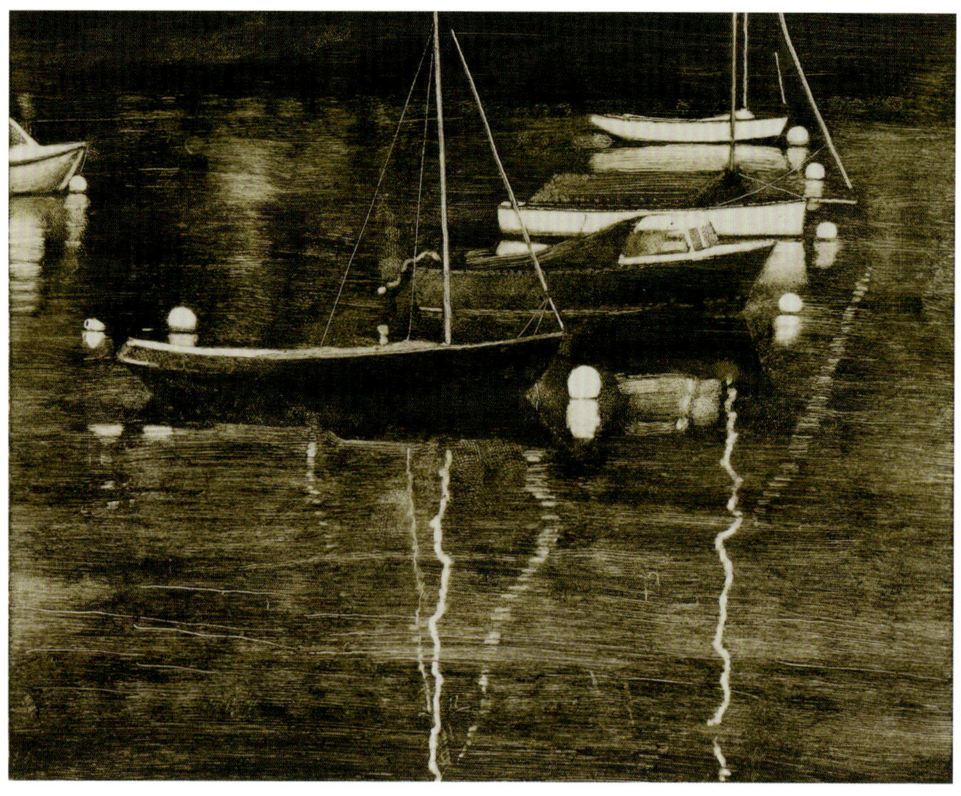

◂ 54 Roseland Peninsula Boats, Incoming Tide II
Monotype on paper
36 x 43 cms 14¼ x 17 ins

▾ 55 Roseland Peninsula Boats, Incoming Tide
Monotype on paper
36 x 43 cms 14¼ x 17 ins

▸ 56 Mousehole Harbour Boats
acrylic on paper
51 x 67 cms 20 x 26¼ ins

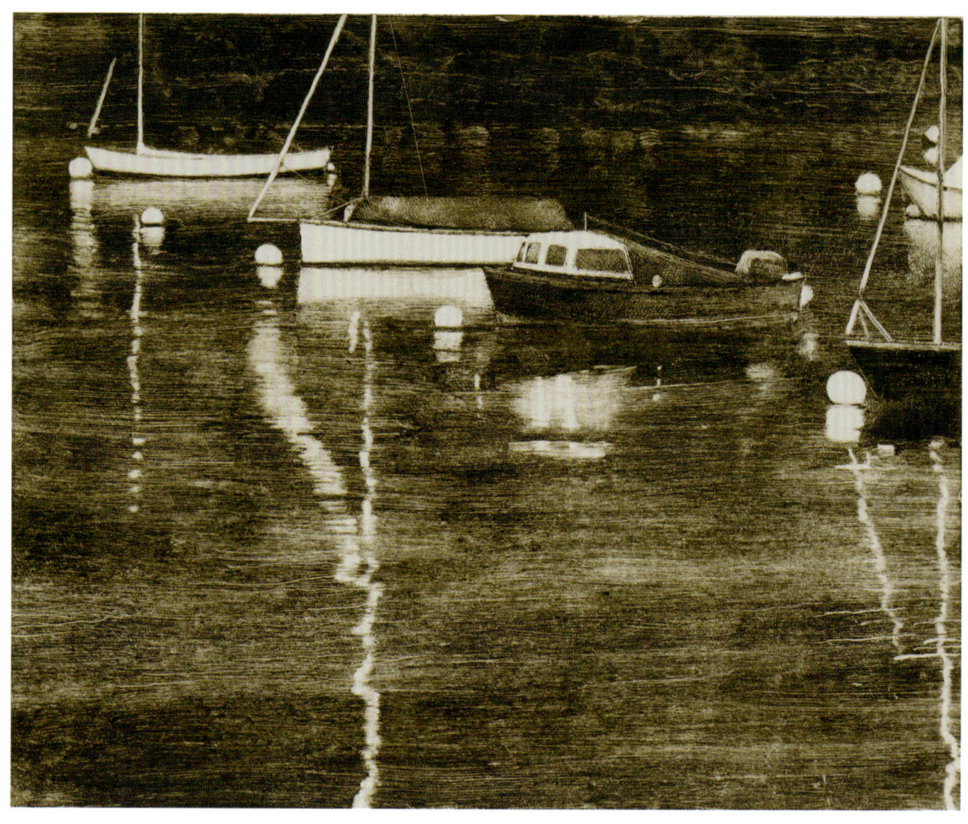

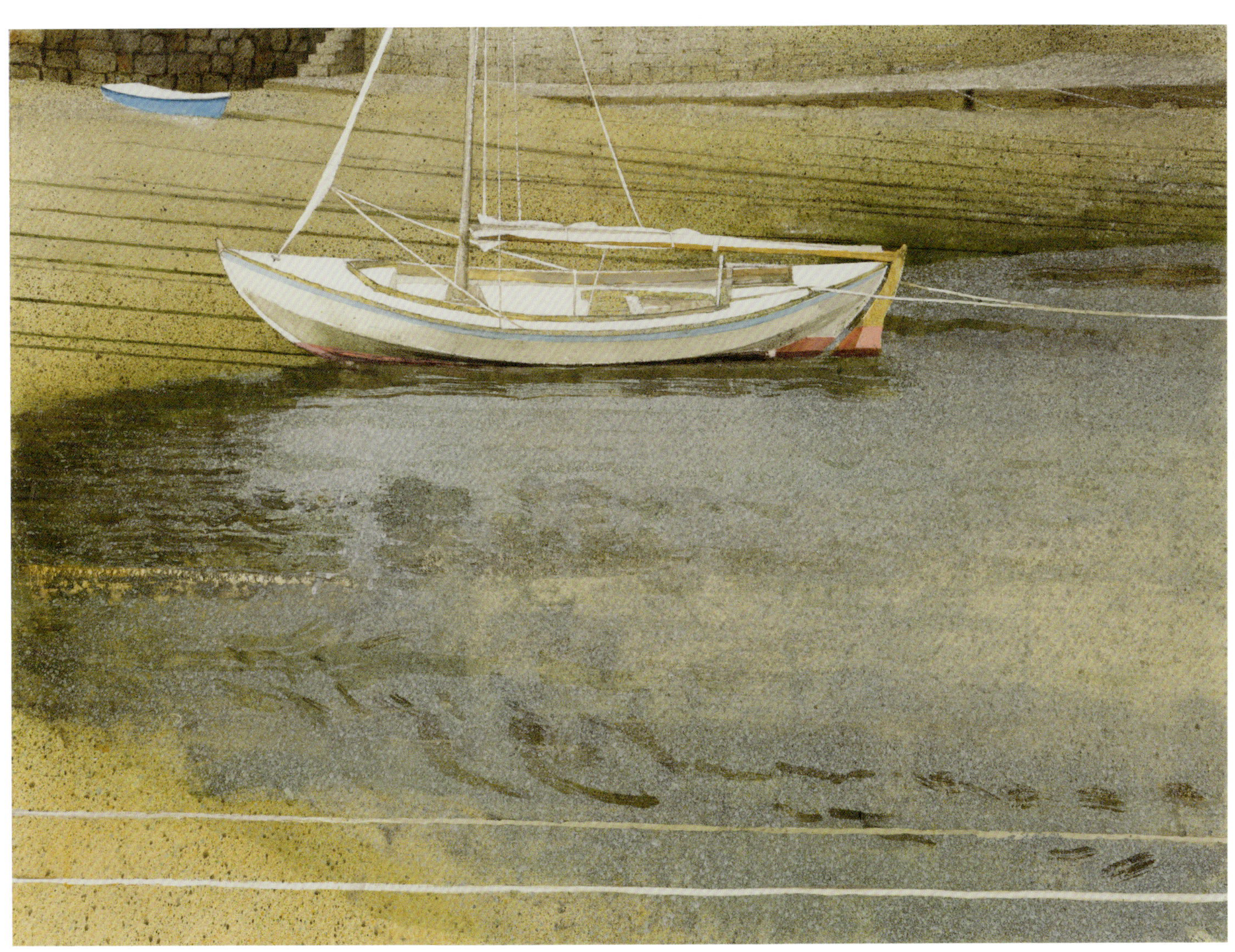

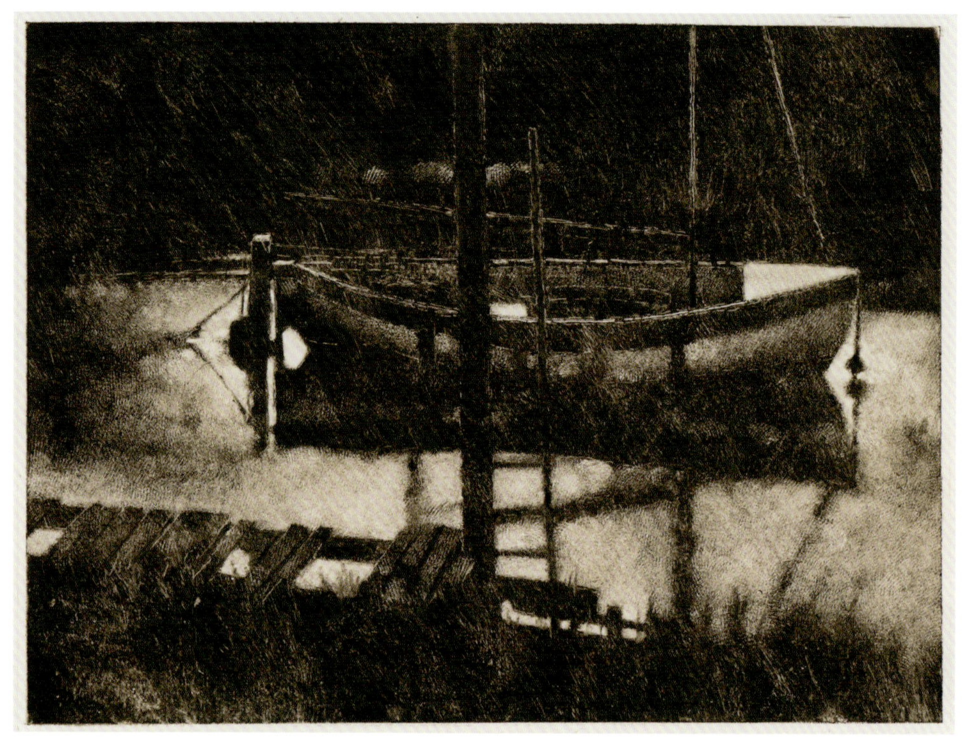

▲ 57 Quayside Boat, Dusk
monotype on Velin Arches cream paper
29 x 38 cms 11½ x 15 ins

▶ 58 Salen Fishing Boats, Isle of Mull
acrylic on canvas on panel
71 x 61 cms 28 x 24 ins

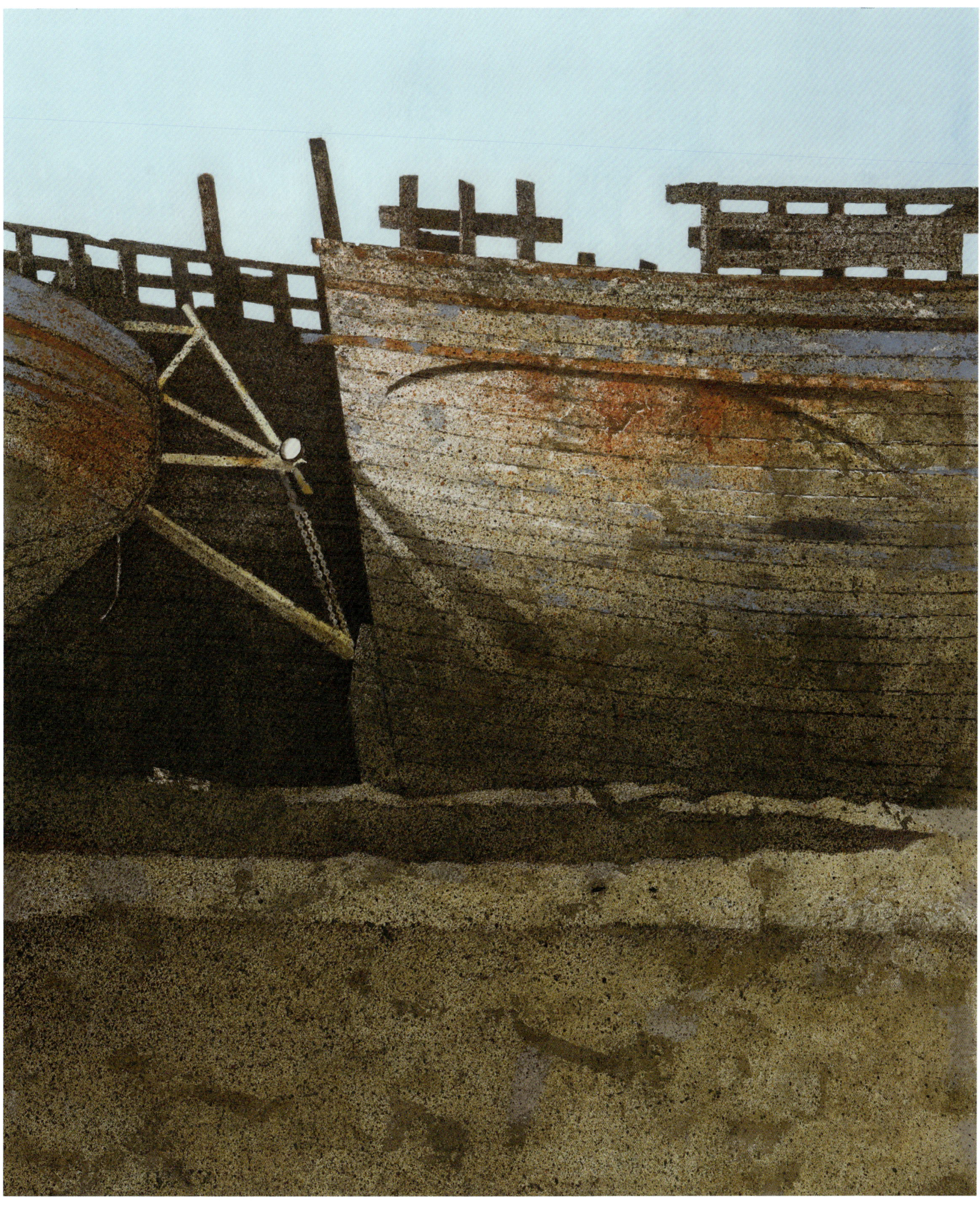

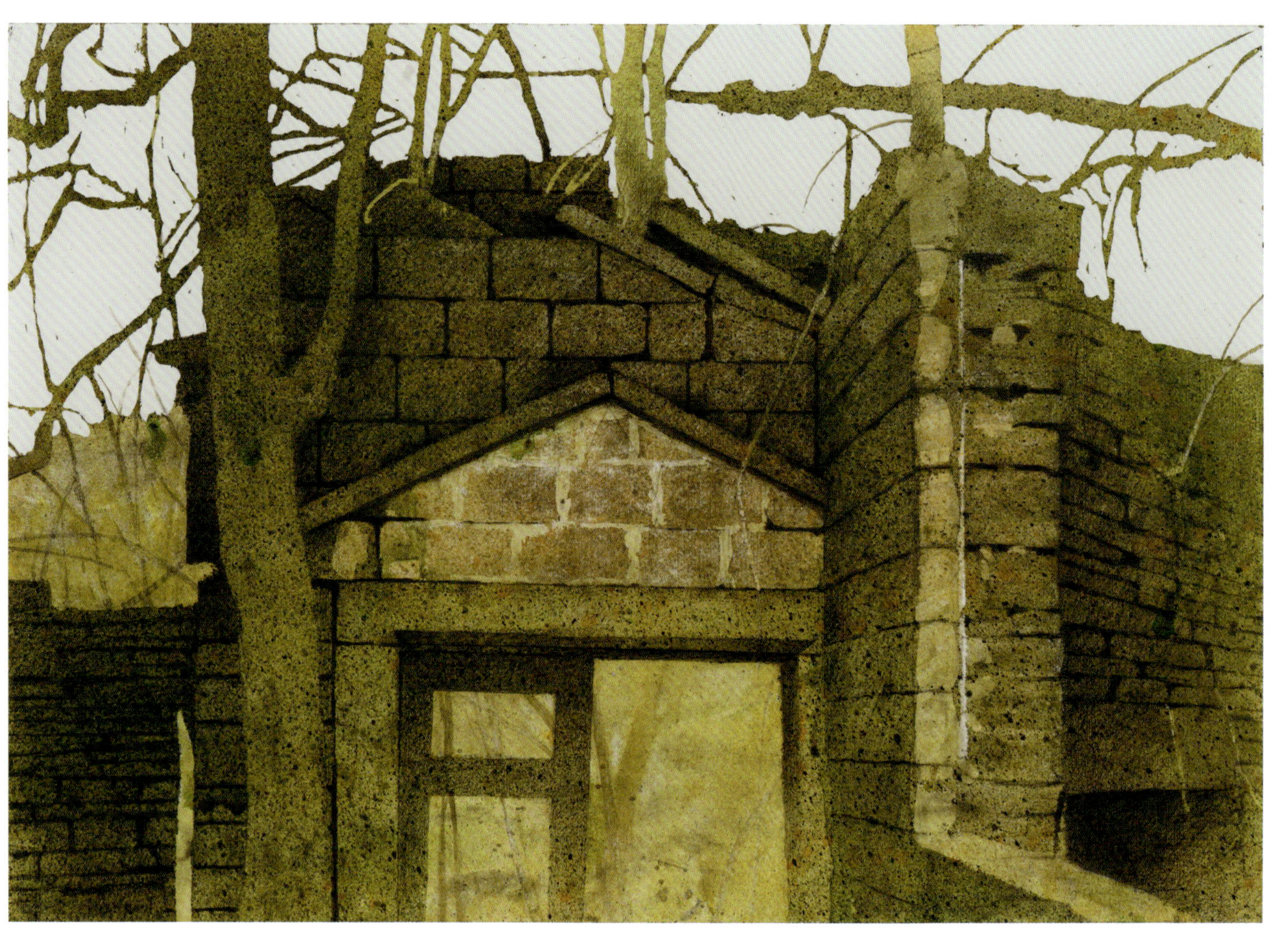

59 Woodland Ruin Near Haworth

acrylic on paper

43 x 60 cms 16¾ x 23½ ins

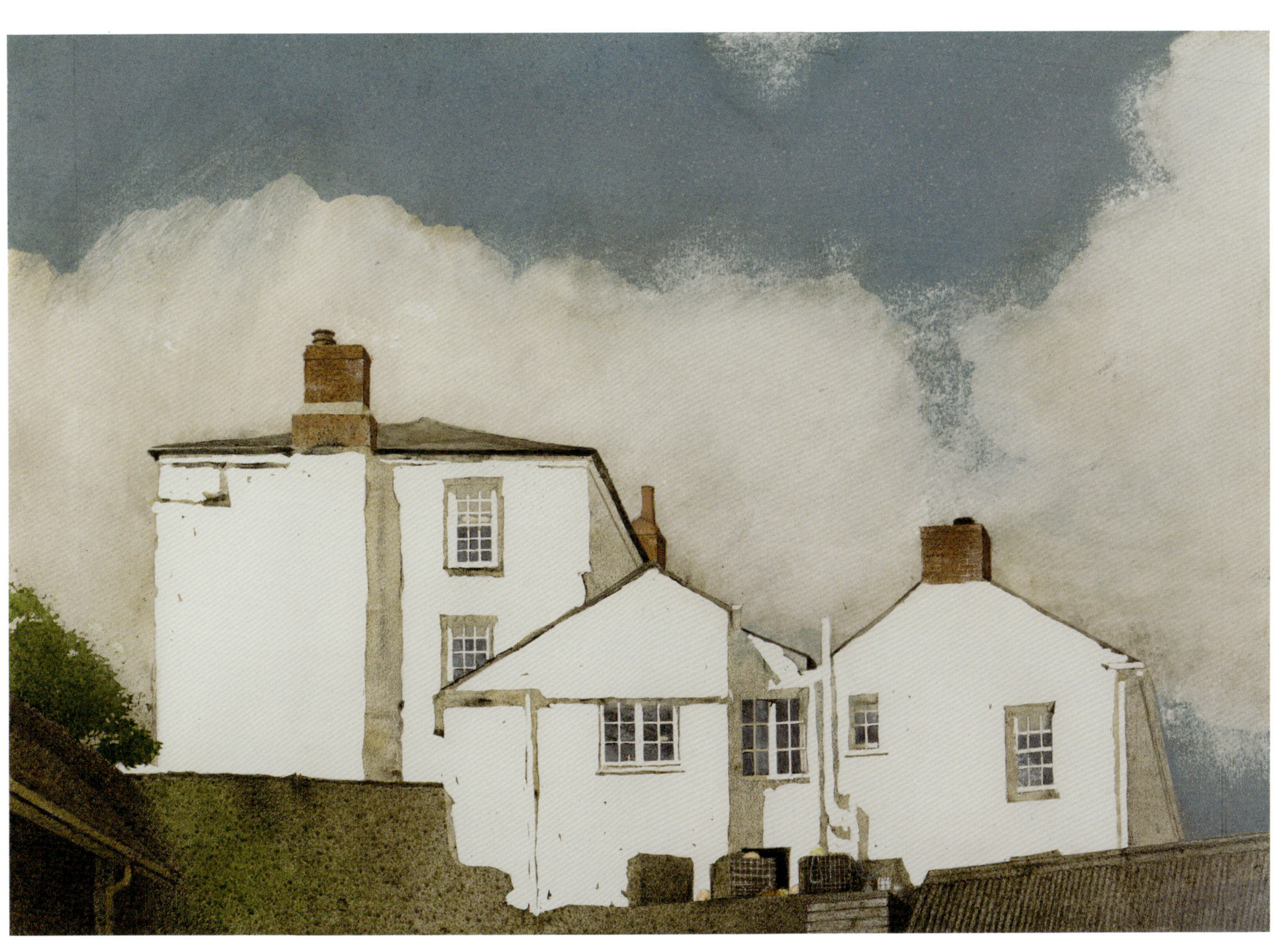

60 Portloe, Bright Morning I
acrylic on paper
50 x 69 cms   19½ x 27¼ ins

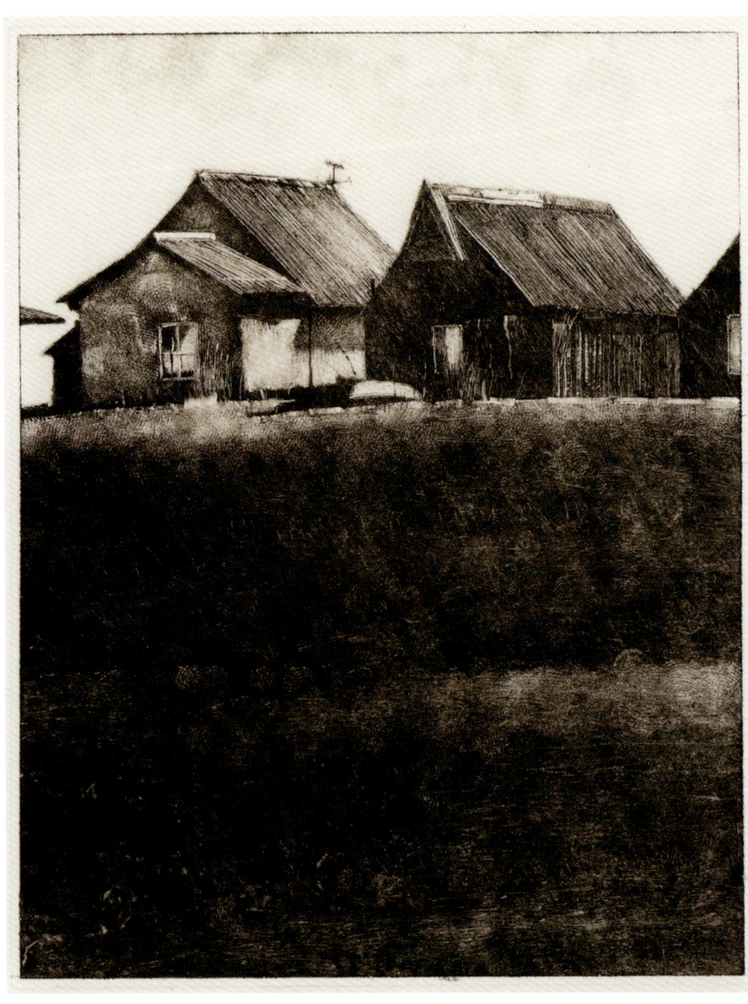

◀ 61 Fisherman's Huts, Southwold II
monotype on Velin Arches cream paper
38 x 29 cms 15 x 11½ ins

▼ 62 Fisherman's Huts, Southwold III
monotype on Velin Arches cream paper
29 x 41 cms 11½ x 16 ins

▶ 63 Polperro Harbour
Monotype on paper
36 x 41 cms 14 x 16¼ ins

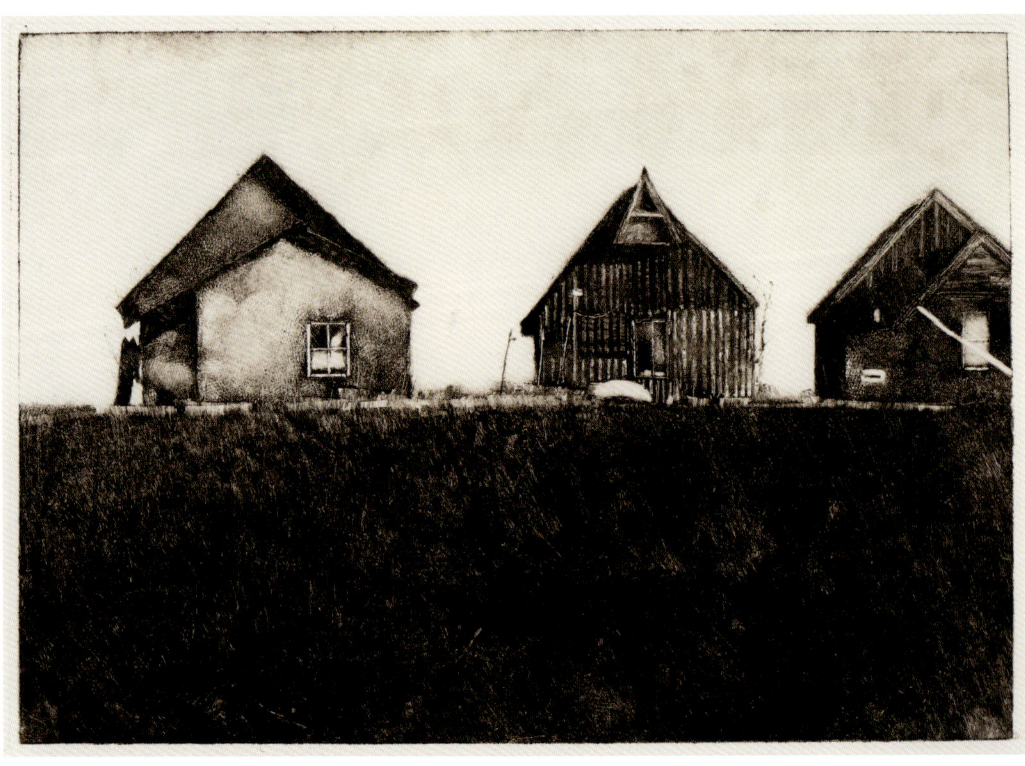

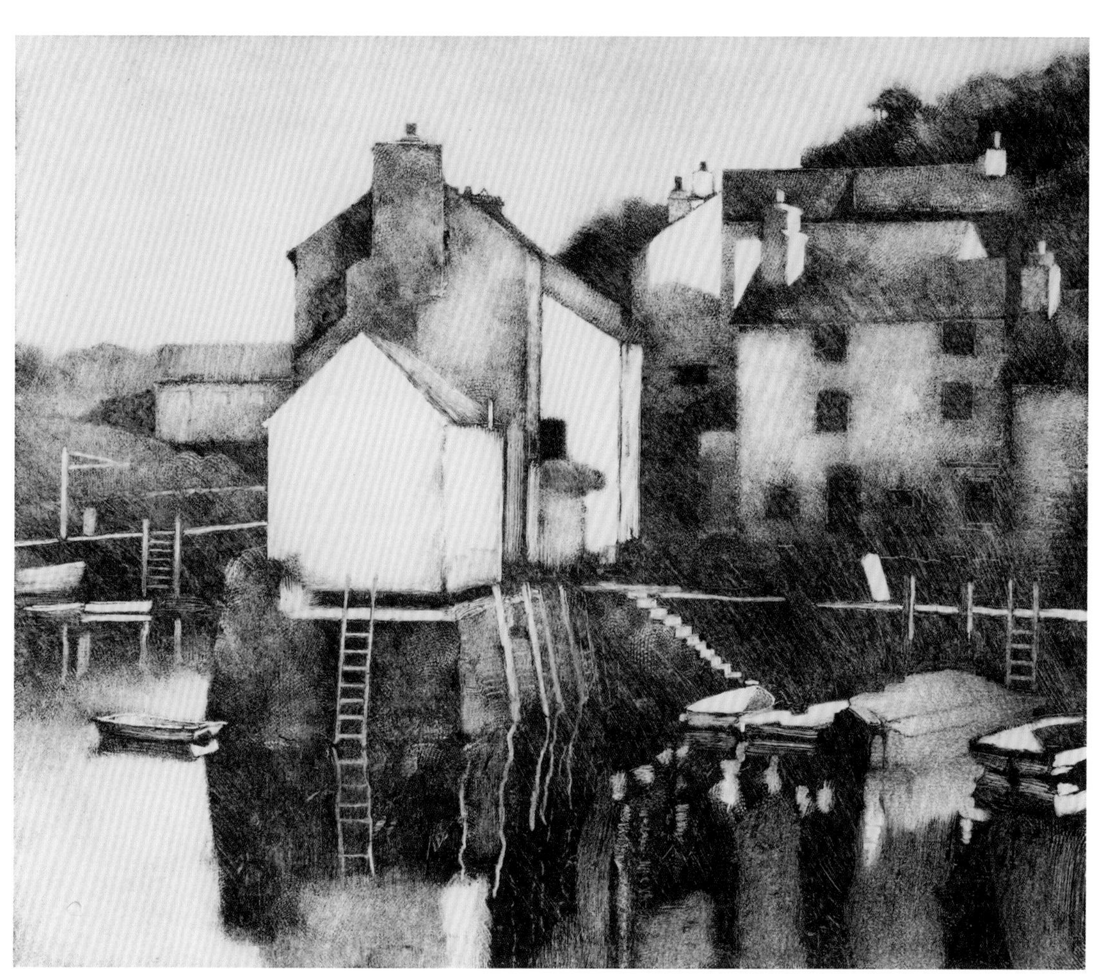

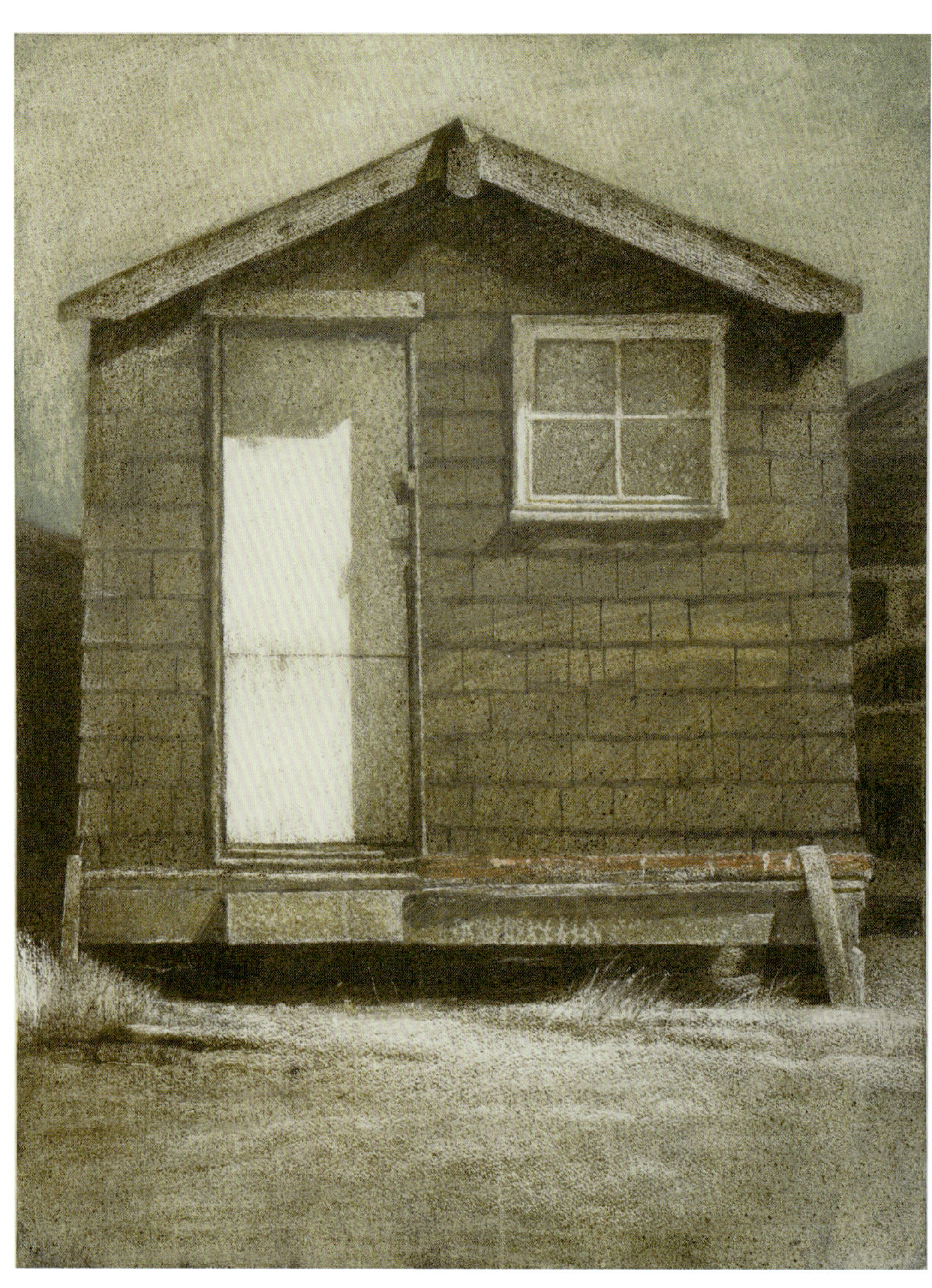

64 Fisherman's Hut

acrylic on Velin Arches cream paper
73 x 54 cms 28¾ x 21¼ ins

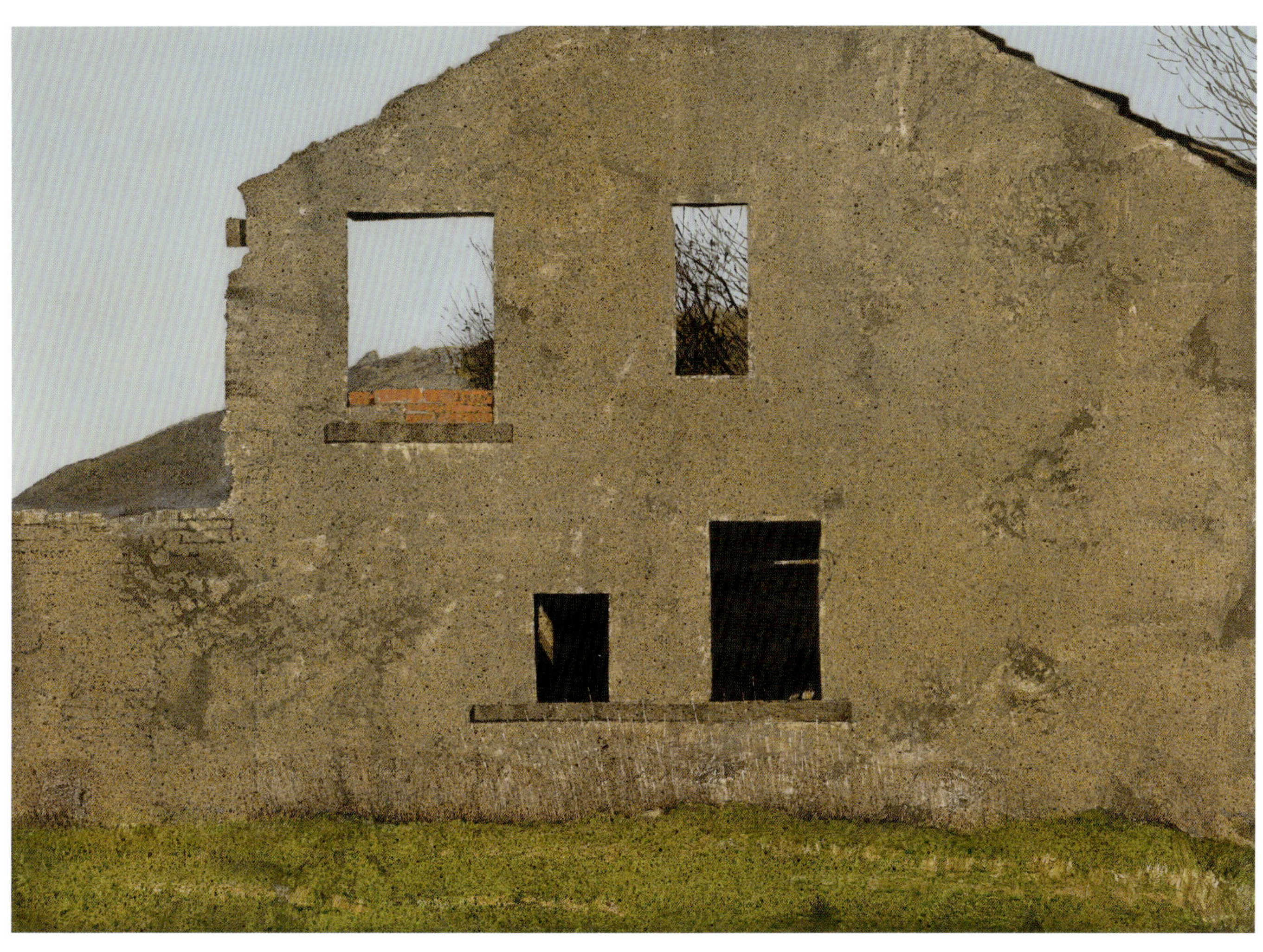

65 Old House Façade, Hills and Trees
acrylic on canvas on panel
55 x 64 cms 21½ x 25 ins

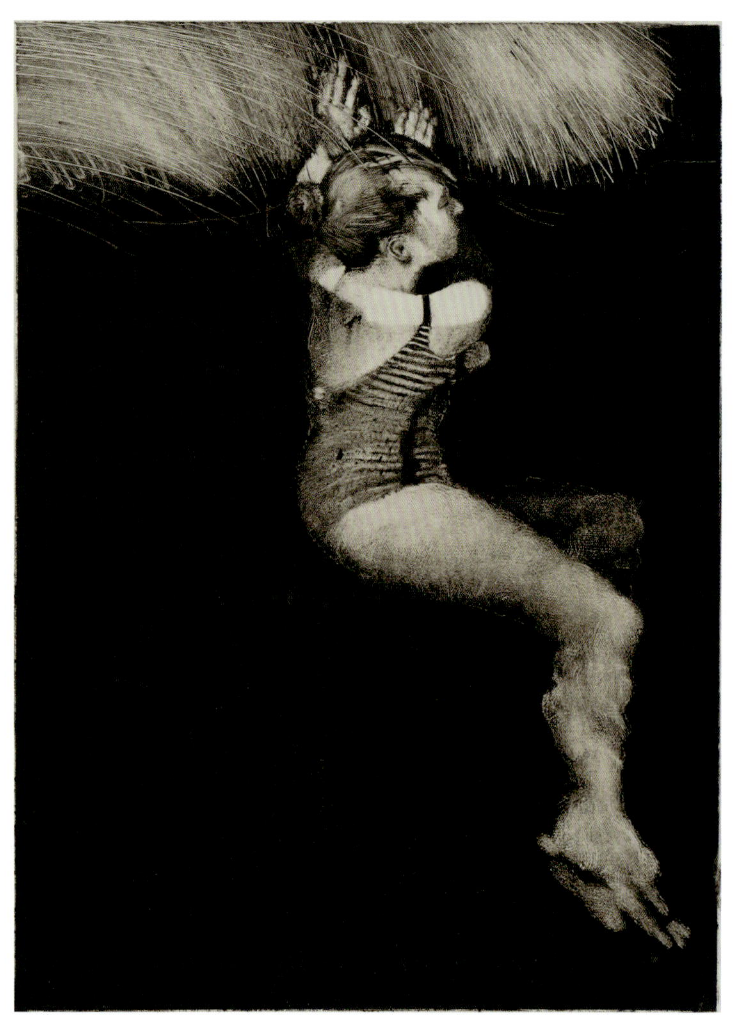

▲ 66 Swimmer in Striped Costume
monotype on Velin Arches cream paper
40 x 29 cms 15¾ x 11⅜ ins

▶ 67 Dye Works Wall with Doorway
acrylic on canvas on panel
86 x 63 cms 33⅞ x 24¾ ins

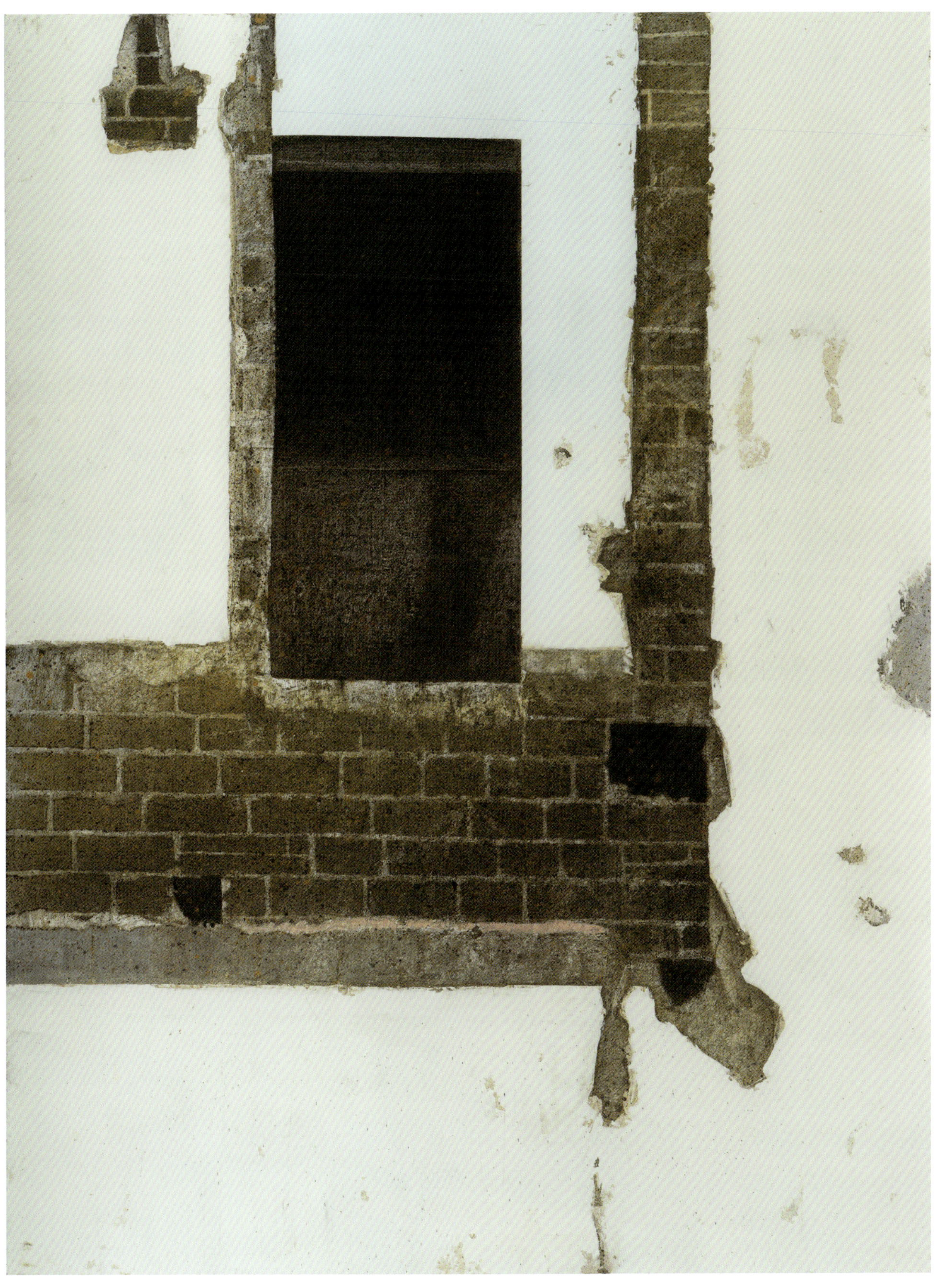

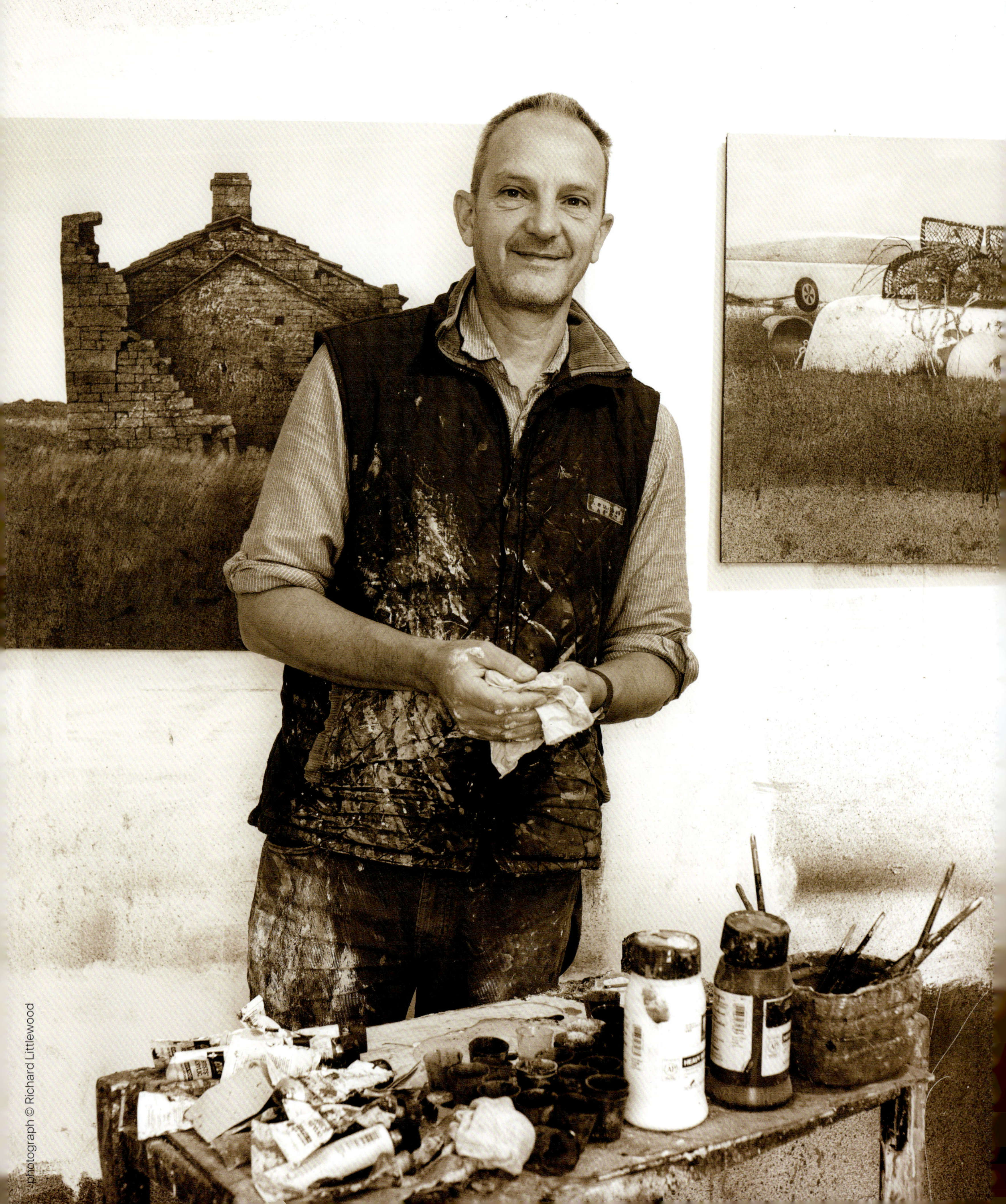

photograph © Richard Littlewood

MAXWELL DOIG

Chronology

1966 Born in Huddersfield, West Yorkshire, UK.

1982–1984 Dewsbury and Batley Art College.

1984 Meets David Blackburn, who becomes a mentor.

1985–1988 Manchester School of Art; awarded BA (Hons) in Fine Art.

1987 Completes first boat drawings, which become an ongoing series.

1988–1990 Slade School of Art; Postgraduate Study in Fine Art.

1989 Anatomy for Artists, University College, London.

1989 Regular visits to British Museum and Petri Museum, UCL.

1990 Commences Association with the Hart Gallery.

1990 First solo exhibition, Hart Gallery, Nottingham. Wins Joseph Webb prize for draughtsman under 35 years.

1991-1992 Awarded place at Hochshule Der Kunst, Berlin, as Artist in Residence. Visits museums and galleries.

1992 Begins to develop methods using mixed media on paper.

1993 Moves to Slaithwaite, near Huddersfield, sets up first studio.

1995 Completes 'Self-portrait drawing textile worker', first aerial view. Shortlisted for Villiers David prize.

1997 Touring exhibition, Wakefield, Harrogate, Salford, Huddersfield. Wins Villiers David Prize. Travels extensively through USA (East and West Coast), Australia and Mexico, visiting anthropology museum in Mexico City and travelling to the Gulf of Mexico.

1998–1999 Completes textural aerial views inspired by travels. Villiers David Prize exhibition, Hart Gallery.

1999–2001 Part-time Lecturer at Leeds Metropolitan University.

2002 Commences Association with the Albemarle Gallery.

2002 First solo exhibition at Albemarle Gallery, London.

2003 Travels to Belgium, visiting museums in Bruges, Brussels and Ghent, seeing works by Van Eyck and Permecke.

2005 First exhibitions in New York and Bologna in association with Albemarle Gallery.

2007 Exhibits in Milan and Bologna. Regular visits to East coast near Whitby.

2008 Solo exhibition, Albemarle Gallery. Continues with aerial views of solitary figures.

2010–2011 'Four British Figurative Painters', Albemarle Gallery and Ettinger Gallery, New York.

2012 Early works from the David Blackburn collection at 108 Gallery, Harrogate.

2013 Solo exhibition at Jersey Arts Centre, St Helier, Jersey.

2014 Making of the film 'Figures in Solitude'.

2015 Solo Exhibition, Albermarle Gallery. Begins to explore architectural ideas.

2017 First solo exhibition at Messum's, Cork Street London.

Second solo exhibition at Huddersfield Art Gallery, entitled "A Sense of Place".

2018 Second solo exhibition at Messum's, Cork Street, London.

2019 Co-curated David Blackburn exhibition at Huddersfield Art Gallery. Travels to the Western Isles.

2020 First solo exhibition at David Messum, St James's, London.

2022 Begins regular trips to the south coast in Devon and Cornwall.

Solo Exhibitions

2025 David Messum Fine Art, St James's, London.

2023 David Messum Fine Art, St James's, London.

2022 David Messum Fine Art, St James's, London.

2020 David Messum Fine Art, St James's, London.

2018 Messum's, Cork Street, London.

2017/18 "A sense of place" Huddersfield Art Gallery.

2017 Messum's, Cork Street, London.

2015 Figures in Solitude, Albermarle Gallery, London

2014 108 Fine Art, Harrogate

2013 Jersey Arts Centre, St Helier, Jersey

2012 Albemarle Gallery, London.

2012 Early Works from the David Blackburn Collection at 108 Fine Art, Harrogate

2008 The Lowry Hotel Manchester

2008 Albemarle Gallery, London

2007 Studio Forni, Milan

2006 Albemarle Gallery, London

2004 Albemarle Gallery, London

2002 Albemarle Gallery, London

2001 Hart Gallery, London

1999 Villiers David Prize Exhibition

1999 Hart Gallery, London

1997 Hart Gallery, London

1997 Touring Exhibition: 'Paintings and Drawings 1987-97', Huddersfield Art Gallery, Wakefield Art Gallery, Mercer Gallery, Harrogate, and Salford Art Gallery

1995 Hart Gallery, London

1994 Hart Gallery, Nottingham

1992 Hart Gallery, Nottingham

1990 Hart Gallery, Nottingham

Selected Group Exhibitions

2025 Modern Romantics, David Messum Fine Art, St James's, London.

2022 The Landscape Renaisance, Messum's Online Studio.

2022 The Elemental North, Messum's Online Studio.

2021 Artists of Fame and of Promise, David Messum Fine Art, St James's, London.

2020 Atelier January 2020, The Studio, Messum's, Marlow.

2019 The Studio, August 2019, Messum's, Marlow.

2018 The Art of Giving, Messum's, Cork Street, London.

2018 Elemental North, Messum's, London.

2018 New Light Prize exhibition, Huddersfield Art Gallery.
2017 New Light Prize exhibition, Bowes Museum.
2016 New Light Prize Open Exhibition, Mercer Gallery Harrogate
2015 New Light Prize Open Exhibition, Bowes Museum, County Durham
2015 Grand Summer Exhibition, Albermarle Gallery, London
2014 Contemporary Realism, Collective Exhibition, Albermarle Gallery, London
2013 Collective Exhibition, Albermarle Gallery, London
2013 Collective Exhibition, Albermarle Gallery, London
2012 Nude Collective Exhibtion, Albermarle Gallery, London
2012 Dive, Art and Water Exhibition, Mercer Gallery, Harrogate
2012 Aqueous Collective Exhibition, Albermarle Gallery, London
2011 Korean Art Fair, Seoul, Albermarle Gallery
2011 Albermarle Gallery, Summer Collective, London
2011 Eleanor Ettinger Gallery, British Figurative Painting, New York
2010 Albermarle Gallery, 4 British Figurative Painters, London
2010 Albermarle Gallery, Charity Group Exhibition, London
2009 Albermarle Gallery, Group Exhibition, London
2008 Albermarle Gallery, Summer Show, London
2007 'Standard Chartered' Exhibition, London
2007 'Form London', Olympia, Albemarle Gallery, London
2007 'Arte Fiera' Galleria Forni, Bologna
2006 'Human Art', Lucio Barbera, Sicily
2006 '10th Anniversary Exhibition', Albemarle Gallery, London
2005 'Arte Fiera' Galleria Forni, Bologna
2005 'Nuovo Figurazione Britannica', Galleria Forni, Bologna
2005 'What is Realism', Albemarle Gallery, London
2005 'Summer Exhibition', Eleanor Ettinger Gallery, New York
2005 'British Figurative Art' Two Man Show, Eleanor Ettinger Gallery, New York
2005 Holman and Fenwick, London
2004 'London Art Fair', Business Design Centre, London
2003 'artLONDON', Burton's Court, London
2003 'Summer Exhibition', Eleanor Ettinger Gallery, New York
2003 'International Sumer Show', Albemarle Gallery, London
2003 'Villiers David Prize-Winners', Ten Years' Christies, London
2003 'New Year, New Work', Albemarle Gallery, London
2000 'Blake's Heaven' Tribute Exhibition to William Blake, Scholar Fine Art
2000 Group Exhibition, Riverhouse Gallery, London
2000 Twentieth Century British Art Fair, London
1999 'Discerning Eye' Exhibition, Mall Galleries, London
1998 Hart Gallery Group Exhibition, Lee & Priestley Solicitors, Leeds
1998 'Art '98' Art Fair, Islington, London
1997 Twentieth Century British Art Fair, London
1997 'Northern Light' Exhibition, Whitehall, London
1996 Twentieth Century British Art Fair, London
1996 'Ghent Art Fair', Hart Gallery Belgium
1995 'Young Masters' Group Exhibition, Mercer Gallery, Harrogate
1995 'Geneva Art Fair', Hart Gallery, Switzerland
1994 Two Man Exhibition, Mercer Gallery, Harrogate
1994 Group Exhibition, Hart Gallery, London
1994 'Art '94', London Art Fair
1993 Group Exhibition, Terrace
1993 Manchester Art Fair
1993 'Laing' Landscape Exhibition, Mall Galleries, London and Mercer Gallery, Harrogate
1992 'Edinburgh Festival, Hart Gallery
1992 'Art '93', London Art Fair
1991 'The Green Book Exhibition', Dean Clough, Halifax
1991 'The Sixth International Art Fair', Olympia, London
1991 Gulascy Gallery, Budapest
1991 'Images of the Yorkshire Landscape', Civic Hall, Leeds
1991 'Post-graduate Exhibition', Slade School of Art
1990 Strang Print Room, University of London
1990 East West Gallery, London
1990 Intaglio Gallery, London
1990 'Bankside Open' Exhibition, London
1989 'Bankside Open' Exhibition, London
1988 'One Hundred and Fifty Years of Art in Manchester', Cavendish Building, Manchester Metropolitan University
1986 'Young Contemporaries', Whitworth Art Gallery, Manchester
1986 Exhibition with Photographer Andrew Sanderson at Huddersfield Sports Centre, opened by Barry Shearman MP

Awards

2015 Shortlisted for the Valeria Sykes Award
1997 Winner of 'Villiers David' Prize
1995 Short-listed for 'Villiers David' Prize
1990 'Joseph Webb' Prize for Draughtsman Under 35 Years
1989 Laura Ashley Scholarship
1988 Scholarship to the Slade School of Art, University of London
1987 Landscape Drawing Award, Manchester Academy Open Exhibition

Selected Essays and Publications

2023 Front cover of quarterly magazine, 'Slightly Foxed', autumn issue no. 79.
2023 'Dartmouth Chronicle', March.

2023 'Kingsbridge and Salcombe Gazette', March.

2023 Messum's catalogue foreword by Patrick Duffy.

2022 Messum's catalogue foreword by David Boyd Haycock.

2022 Country Life, Art Market Overview by Huon Mallaleui.

2020 Messum's catalogue foreword by David Boyd Haycock

2018 Messum's catalogue foreword by David Boyd Haycock.

2018 Pick of the Week, Art Market by Huon Mallalieu, September, Country Life magazine.

2018 'My Yorkshire' double page spread Yorkshire Post magazine, 13th January.

2018 Feature in *Artist & Illustrators* magazine, January.

2017 Feature by Andrew Hirst, Huddersfield Examiner, November.

2017 Feature by Hilary Stelfox, Huddersfield Examiner, January.

2017 Messum's catalogue introduction by Andrea Gates.

2015 'Maxwell Doig Disegno and a sense of decorum' essay by Robert Hall (art historian and curator).

2015 'The Silence of Solitude: The Vision of Maxwell Doig', Catalogue essay by Lynne Green

2013 'Studio Visit' critical essay by Jo Manby

2013 Ithaca Lit, Spring. Featured artist by Michelle Lesko

2012 'The Art of the Nude' by John O'Hern, *Amercian Art Collector* magazine, October 2012

2012 Feature by Val Javin, September, *Huddersfield Examiner*

2012 In Conversation with Andrew Stewart, Exhibition Catalogue

2011 Exhibition review, 'British Figurative Painting' at Ettinger Gallery, New York, *American Arts Quarterly*, Summer 2011, Volume 28, No 3.

2008 Exhibition review by Steve Pil for *Artists & Illustrators*, May

2007 Catalogue essay by Barbara Frigario, 'Figures in Solitude'.

2007 Exhibition review by Alessandro Redaelli for *Art* magazine, October

2006 Catalogue essay by John Russell Taylor, solo exhibition, Albemarle Gallery.

2006 Book cover: *The Novel Now* by Richard Bradford (Oxford: Blackwell)

2005 Interview with Jenny Parkin for *Huddersfield Examiner* 11th February.

2003 *Who's Who in Art*, 31st Edition, Hilmarton Manor Press

2003 Christies exhibition review 'Formal & Dignified' by Tim Forrest, *Mayfair Life*, August

2001 Exhibition review by Elspeth Moncrieff for *The Art Newspaper*, No. 114, May

2001 Front cover, *Galleries* magazine with painting 'Warehouse Roof'.

2001 'Profile' by Joe Manby in *Arts Review*, May

2000 Book cover: *Blue Fever* by Clare MacDonald Shaw (Blackwater Press)

1999 Exhibition review by John Russell Taylor for *The Times*, 19 January

1999 Exhibition review by Charlotte Mullins for *Galleries*, January

1998 'Sense and Sensation', article by Huon Mallalieu for *Country Life*, June

1998 Featured artist, 'i2i', artist newsletter, in conversation with Kirsty McGee. Touring exhibition review, 'City Life', Manchester by Kirsty McGee, April.

1998 Catalogue essay for 'Villiers David' Prize Exhibition, by Bridget Hayden

1997 Catalogue essay by Charlotte Mullins for touring exhibition.

1997 Exhibition review by Bridget Hayden for the *Big Issue*

1997 Exhibition review by Deborah Stone for the *Daily Express*

1995 Provident Financial Art Collection Catalogue: *A Celebration of 25 Years of Collecting*, critical assessment by John Sheeran

1995 Book cover: *In a Rare Time of Rain* by Milner Place (London: Chatto & Windus)

1995 Publication of essays: *The Gaze of Love: Meditations on Art* by Sister Wendy Beckett (London: Marshall Pickering)

1994 Exhibition review by Mary Sara for the *Yorkshire Post*

1993 'A Poetic Dialogue: Seven Painters', The Hart Gallery

1991 Illustrated essay by Malcolm York for the *Green Book*

1990 Catalogue introduction by David Blackburn, intro by John Hart

Collections

Jersey Arts Centre

Standard Chartered

Holman and Fenwick

University of London

Mercer Gallery, Harrogate

Provident Financial Group

Huddersfield Art Gallery

Prudential plc

New Light

Works in private collections throughout the UK, Europe and USA

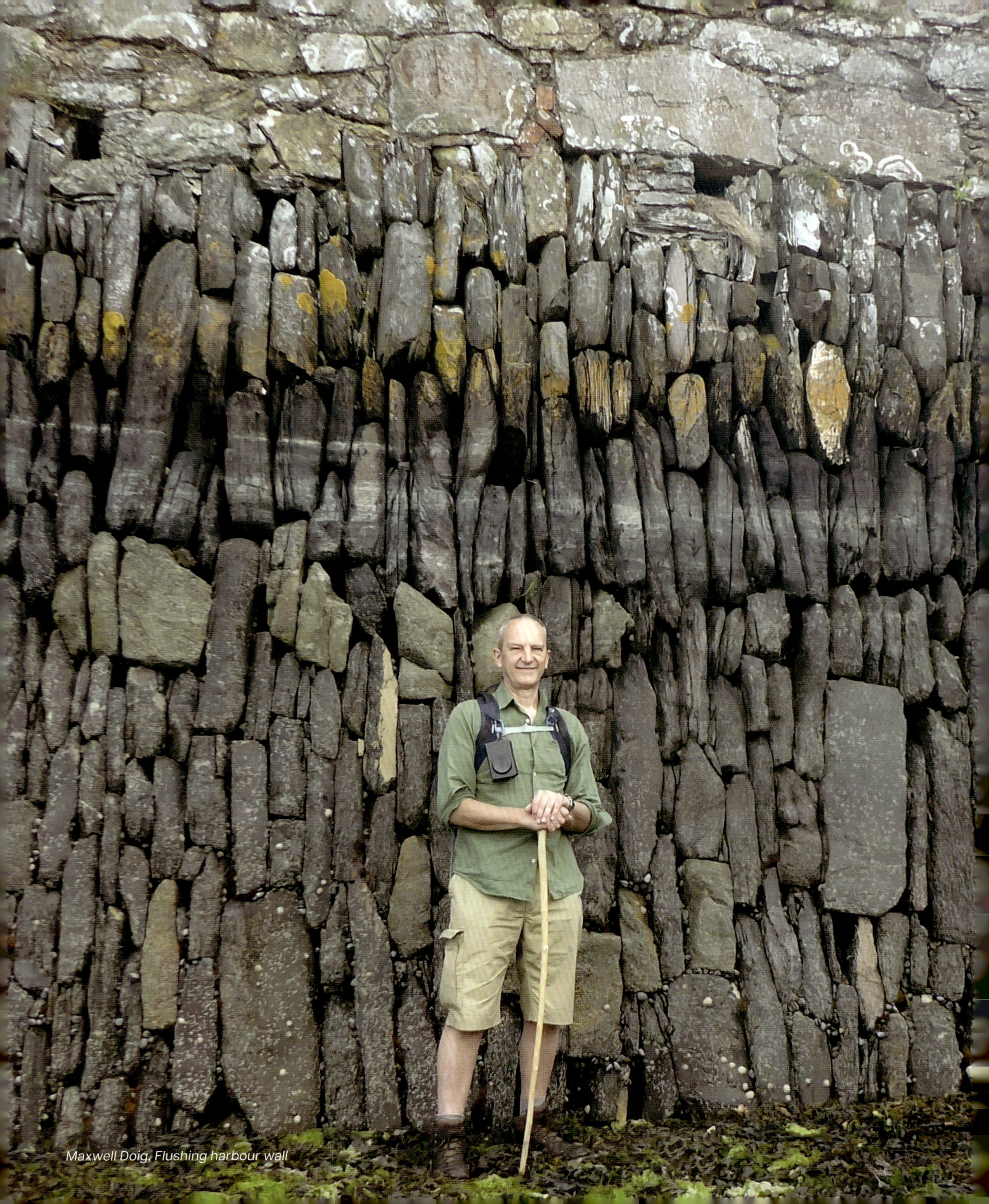
Maxwell Doig, Flushing harbour wall